Lessons from the XKE

As the details and opinions circulate of the sale of Jaguar and Land Rover to the massive Tata conglomerate in India, optimists and naysayers alike rushed to express an opinion. Blog sites swelled with comments, pro and con. It occurred to me that a look back into the history of Jaguar, specifically that of the XKE, might hold some lessons for contemporary consideration by the new owners.

The last E-type Jaguar rolled off the Coventry assembly line in 1974, ending a production run of 14 years that gave the world one of the most beautiful automobiles in history. Here was a car that could do an honest 150 mph without the stratospheric price tag of its Italian cousins; it consistently earned its stripes on the racing circuit as well. In contrast to the lackluster financial contributions of the current Jaguar line, the XKE contributed handsomely to the coffers of British Leyland during its production run.

While the XKE was a truly beautiful car that still turns heads, it was fundamentally a car engineered

> *"I believe one can validly pose the question: Has there ever been a car so widely perceived to be so exceptionally beautiful as the E-type?"*
>
> -Malcolm Sayers, 1916-1970
> Designer, Director-Jaguar, New Product Design

with aerodynamic efficiency, the result of continual tweaking as information filtered in from racing experience. XKE chief engineer William Heynes noted, "It would be true to say that the E-type is almost completely a product of our racing experience. We have built into this a body shape which has been improved and improved, both in wind tunnels and in really high speed tests, and it would be no idle claim to say that it has a lower drag figure per square foot of frontal area than any other car at present in production."

And that's my point. Jaguar doesn't need customers, it needs devotees who appreciate performance, design, style and efficiency. There is no substitute for the

R&D contribution of a racing program to provide well tested solutions to the problems that show up during the rigors of racing. Whether the final product is a sports car, luxury sedan or fuel-efficient hybrid, it should have a racing program as a bedrock requirement.

Automotive history tells us that, like Darwinian natural selection, marques come and go. True enough. Over the course of the past 100 years or so, it's estimated that more than 5,000 car companies have thrown their hat in the ring while only a handful survive today.

Admittedly, it's a tough, competitive jungle out there. However, Jaguar is one cat we'd like to keep. Tata, here's your chance.

Drive in Peace,

Gerry Durnell
Editor & Publisher

Automobile Quarterly

The Connoisseur's Publication of Motoring
– Today, Yesterday, and Tomorrow –

GERRY DURNELL
Editor & Publisher

KAYE BOWLES-DURNELL
Associate Publisher

JOHN C. DURNELL
Chief Operations Officer, Technical Editor

TRACY POWELL
Managing Editor

JOHN EVANS
Chief Financial Officer

DAN BULLEIT
Art Director

ROD HOTTLE
Administrative Assistant

ROBIN JEFFERS
Customer Service

L. SCOTT BAILEY
Founding Editor and Publisher

Contributing Photographers
GAVIN FARMER
MARIO LAGUNA
STUDIO PASCUCCI

Contributing Writers
ANDREW BECKMAN
BROOKS T. BRIERLEY
RIC A. DIAS
GAVIN FARMER
PATRICK FOSTER
MARIO LAGUNA
L. SPENCER RIGGS

www.autoquarterly.com

ISBN 1-59613-057-1
(978-1-59613-057-9)

Printed in Korea

1964 PORSCHE 35

S/N: 217963
BIRTH DATE / PRODUCTION COMPLETION DATE: 05/08/1964
ENGINE NUMBER: 811839
TRANSMISSION NUMBER: 77802
EXT: SIGNAL RED #6407
INT: BLACK LEATHER
OPTIONAL EQUIPMENT:
"DUNLOP" TIRES
2 HEADRESTS
CHROME WHEELS
COMPENSATING SPRING
OWNER: HANK WEIL

C KARMANN COUPE

Contents

VOLUME 48, NUMBER 1 • FIRST QUARTER 2008

Cover: Illustration by Steve Anderson

STUDEBAKER'S FINAL DAYS
1952-1970

I t has been said that all changes, even the most longed for, have their melancholy. This sentiment is certainly the case with Studebaker, whose last years of life were a whirlwind of success and failure.

BY PATRICK FOSTER

Commander V-8 Starliner "hard-top" convertible.

Chrome wheel discs optional at extra cost—decorative and other specifications subject to change without notice.

Studebaker again steps out ahead in style

HERE it is—the exciting new Studebaker styling that is the talk of the entire nation.

Here's glamor beyond words—distinction beyond question—in new Studebakers paced by the most beautiful "hard-top" in America.

Stop in right away at a nearby Studebaker showroom and arrange to try out one of these eagerly responsive, amazingly thrifty Studebaker style stars.

Studebaker's the newest of the new for '52—a sprightly new Studebaker Champion in the lowest price field—a brilliant-performing new 120-horsepower Studebaker Commander V-8.

See Studebaker for '52

Studebaker, South Bend 27, Indiana, U. S. A.

Sparkling with eye appeal—the dramatically styled 1952 Studebaker Champion, or Commander V-8, four-door sedan.

In 1966 Studebaker – America's oldest transportation company – closed its remaining automobile plant and exited the car business. The most bewildering thing of all is how quickly the company fell apart. After all, this was no insignificant startup company – Studebaker was more than a century old and once was America's largest independent automaker. The company was in business a full 50 years before it produced its first automobile in 1902. At Studebaker's 100th anniversary in 1952 it lagged just behind the Big Three. Just 11 years later, its huge manufacturing complex in South Bend, Ind., closed for good.

The post-WWII era had started out well. Studebaker was the first company to introduce an all-new postwar model in 1946, management believing the company "stood to gain much from being the first to give its customers the advantage of advancements both in design and production." The advanced styling of Studebaker's new envelope-body cars was impressive, with fenders integrated into the design rather than looking added on. Buyers waited in line for a glimpse.

In the postwar era, Studebaker began to establish a reputation as a leader in automobile styling. The radical bulletnose Studebakers of 1950 showed how far the company was willing to go in vehicle design. Although this design sold very successfully, Studebaker's boldness backfired in 1953 when the public rejected the newly styled sedans.

The company soon built a reputation for styling. The 1950 Studebaker introduced controversial frontal styling with rounded fenders flanking a bullet-nose. Some thought it was the look of the future, others hated it, but it was very successful. In 1951 the company brought out a new V8 engine years before Nash, Hudson, Packard and even Pontiac.

Then came Studebaker's centennial in 1952, a year-long celebration for the company. There was much to be proud of. Studebaker was one of the largest automakers in the world and the future looked bright. The 1952 cars were face-lifted by Raymond Loewy's designers, featuring a sloping hood and low-set grille that successfully blended the existing lines with a preview of styling themes that would debut on the all-new '53 Studebakers.

But business results for 1952 were mixed. Sales of $586 million were a new record, and net income rose 13 percent to $14.2 million. But profits were far lower than 1948, 1949 or 1950 despite greater sales volume. The problem was high labor costs and low productivity, which had taken root during WWII's huge demand for military products. Postwar conditions only exacerbated the problem. With the public clamoring for new cars, management wouldn't risk a strike, caving in to wage demands and turning a blind eye to low productivity. By 1952 work standards at Studebaker were said to be among the lowest in the industry.

The soaring postwar demand for autos suddenly ended. Studebaker introduced all-new cars that year, and they proved the company's undoing. Originally, the 1953 Studebakers were to have conventional styling. However, Raymond Lowey convinced management to authorize production of a stylish coupe with low-slung, very European styling. But then stylists went back and redesigned the sedans to incorporate elements of the coupe styling and that proved a colossal mistake – the awkward Euro-styling made the cars look small. While public reaction to the "Loewy" coupe was outstanding, response to the new Commander and Champion sedans was tepid. Another problem was the discovery that the sales division had badly underestimated expected demand for the coupes while overestimating sedan sales. Also hampering sales were production delays caused by front-end sheet metal that would not mate to the body.

This all cost a great many sales, and Studebaker lost money on car production during the first quarter of 1953. April was profitable but in May production had to be cut when a supplier went on strike. Just as that problem was fixed Ford launched its historic Blitz,

There were only minor changes to the Studebaker from 1953 (above) to the following year's model. The 1954 Commander Starlight coupe shown below came standard with a V8 engine in addition to gorgeous styling.

an attempt to wrest sales leadership from Chevrolet's grasp. Ford factories shipped thousands of extra cars to dealers, forcing retailers to sell cars for a few dollars over invoice to clear the glut. Chevrolet followed suit and the two giants became locked in a battle that decimated Studebaker. Profits fell more than 80 percent to $2.68 million.

Studebaker's only real product news for 1954 was the Conestoga station wagon, long overdue and unfortunately offering only two doors just as the market was turning to four-door wagons. As the competitor blitz continued, the company's financial condition worsened, and wage problems could no longer be ignored. In early 1954 the union signed an agreement providing the company some relief. But Studebaker continued to sink, losing $8.3 million in the first quarter. Production went into freefall, dropping to 113,920 vehicles in 1954 versus 334,554 in 1950.

A merger with Packard appeared to be the only solution. Packard and Studebaker combined would cover nearly every market segment. And if they could produce Studebaker, Packard and Clipper cars on a common body shell, tooling and amortization costs would be sharply reduced.

Neither Studebaker nor Packard looked very promising on paper. Studebaker was losing money at a frightening pace, and although Packard was in better shape financially, it too was losing money. Both companies hoped to avoid having their books closely examined, so an agreement was reached that each would supply the other with the necessary figures on costs, breakeven, net worth and other figures.

They merged on Oct. 1, 1954, with former Packard chief James Nance as president. Studebaker-Packard Corporation was the fourth largest automaker in America with more than 4,000 dealers, two automobile brands, trucks and substantial military business. Nance guessed the firm would lose $9 million in 1955, post a smaller loss for 1956 and record a handsome profit in 1957 with all-new cars on a shared body.

Worried about continuing losses at Studebaker, Nance sent finance VP Walter Grant to South Bend to get a handle on Studebaker's costs. A shocked Grant discovered that the 165,000-unit breakeven point mentioned in talks was all wrong – Studebaker's actual breakeven was 282,000 cars. Nance probably wished he had insisted on a complete audit of Studebaker's books prior to the merger, instead of choosing to neglect fiduciary responsibilities in order to speed things up.

The result showed at year's end when the company reported an operating loss of $41.7 million, reduced to a net loss of $26 million after tax credits. Until something was done to correct Studebaker's problems of poor sales and low productivity the bleeding would continue.

The 1955 Studebakers were only mildly face-lifted with a taller hood line and a heavy chrome grille replacing the 1954's twin grilles. A new top-line 120.5-inch wheelbase President series debuted offering two sedans, a coupe and a hardtop plus the gorgeous President Speedster hardtop sporting simulated wire wheels, bumperettes with fog lights, and beautiful interior trim. Sales rose slightly to

Above: The 1954 Studebaker Conestoga station wagon. Below: Although they looked small compared to the competition, the 1956 Studebakers offered decent styling and good value. Shown is the new President Classic four-dour sedan. Opposite: The 1956 Sky Hawk.

Studebaker *Champion Scotsman* 2-Door

Full Size...Full Power...Maximum Economy

This new 2-door Champion Scotsman has everything! Crisp, clean design ... full size ... full power ... full comfort ... PLUS new three-way economy. (1) *Economy when you buy* ... a price so surprisingly low ... yet it includes such extra equipment as a heater/defroster, directional signals, spare wheel and tire— everything you need for safety and comfort. (2) *Economy while you drive* ... up to 29 miles per gallon of gasoline with all other operating costs to match. (3) *Economy when you trade* ... a proven fact based on Studebaker's historically higher resale values. For your only car ... for your extra car ... the Champion Scotsman is today's best value ... a car that's smart to purchase, a car you can drive with pride.

Functional Interior...More Headroom...Front and Rear

This is an interior built for hard family use ... style-wise beauty combined with durability. You'll appreciate its value as weeks of daily use grow into months and into years. You'll also enjoy the extra headroom built into this car, front and rear, every day you drive your Scotsman.

138,742 cars and trucks versus 113,920 the prior year – better, but because 1955 was a record year for the industry, it wasn't very impressive. The business lost another $29.7 million.

Although the company desperately needed to consolidate Studebaker, Packard and Clipper models on a shared body, no lender was willing to provide the funding. So restricted, the best Studebaker could afford for 1956 was an extensive facelift, sedans and wagons looking more conventional with new fenders, hood and deck lid. Stylists turned the coupe/hardtop body into a new sporty car called the Hawk. The line included a six-cylinder Flight Hawk coupe, a V8 Power Hawk coupe and Skyhawk hardtop and, topping the line, the awesome Golden Hawk hardtop powered by a 352-cid Packard V8.

But buyer response to the 1956 line was only fair and production dropped to roughly 82,000 cars and 20,000 trucks. Studebaker-Packard recorded an operating loss of $43.7 million plus $60 million in special charges for inventory obsolescence and writing down the Packard plants, for a net loss of $102.3 million. The company was dying.

Nance talked with International Harvester, Curtiss-Wright, Chrysler and others about merging or selling assets. Defense supplier Curtiss-Wright was the only one interested, attracted mainly by factories like the modern Utica, Mich., plant where jet engines and Packard V8s were built. Curtiss-Wright president Roy Hurley knew that if he merged, Studebaker-Packard's prior losses could provide tax write-offs on his future profits. Realizing he had Nance over a barrel Hurley toyed with him, first saying he wanted to merge, then calling it off, stringing things along as S-P's cash melted away. Hurley demanded huge military orders from the government, which didn't want S-P to fail, in exchange for helping bail out the company. The hard-nosed tactics worked: Hours before Studebaker-Packard was ready to declare insolvency, a deal was reached.

Curtiss-Wright gave Studebaker-Packard $10 million for its defense business and $25 million to lease its Utica and Chippewa plants for 12 years. Hurley wouldn't merge though, agreeing only to manage S-P

Above: America's lowest-priced full-size car for 1957 was this Studebaker Scotsman two-door sedan. Essentially, it was a Champion stripped of all chrome and extras, though a heater/defroster was standard. Below: The company managed to cobble together a Packard for 1957 by applying Packard's 1956 styling themes to a Studebaker President. The result was not bad looking—but it wasn't a Packard. Opposite: The 1957 Golden Hawk.

Model year 1958 brought another facelift of the sadly out-of-date body. Stylists grafted small pods onto the front fenders to fit quad lamps, considered necessary to be contemporary. They came standard on Commander and President, optional on Champion. A stylish new hardtop debuted and the utilitarian Scotsman returned. The company did its best to sell the slightly warmed over cars but it was difficult to compete against competitors' larger, newer-looking cars. Additionally, buyers' fears of owning an orphan was a very significant problem.

During the first nine months of 1958 sales fell to $92 million, and the company recorded a loss of $22 million. However, hope began to rise during the last

Above: The Studebaker Golden Hawk for 1957 continued to thrill enthusiasts with its power and handling capabilities. Right: The company managed to introduce one new body style for 1958, this two-door hardtop President. The new hardtop was also available in the Commander series.

for three years at cost in exchange for an option on five million shares of stock. That way Hurley could run Studebaker-Packard as he wanted without actually taking a financial stake in the firm. If he saved it he could exercise his stock option, buy the company and use S-P tax credits to offset C-W profits. If Studebaker-Packard failed, his own company would not suffer. It was the sort of deal only a desperate company like Studebaker-Packard would agree to. The company also agreed to distribute Mercedes-Benz cars in North America. Hurley felt having another line to sell would strengthen the retail network.

If Studebaker-Packard had been able to use the cash influx to immediately bring out all-new cars, they might have been able to turn things around, but Hurley's negotiating tactics had wasted a great deal of time. All that 1957 offered was yet another revision of the unsuccessful 1953 cars. The results could have been predicted.

The 1957 models were mildly face-lifted, and a four-door station wagon was finally added to the line-up. The Silver Hawk coupe offered either six or eight cylinders while the mighty Golden Hawk hardtop now offered a 275hp supercharged Studebaker V8. The cars were solid values and the styling was decent, but

they came about two years too late to do much good. Packard production was transferred to South Bend and stylists cobbled together a 1957 Packard Clipper by applying 1956 Packard styling cues to the Studebaker President. Fewer than 5,000 were sold.

Noticing the success of import cars, S-P's new president Harold Churchill wondered if perhaps a low-price full-size car would attract buyers. In mid-1957 he introduced the Scotsman, a line of Champion-based cars stripped to the basics. They were terribly plain cars, but with prices starting at $1,776, they sold fairly well. Losses, however, continued. For 1957 the company lost $11 million.

quarter. The management agreement with Curtis-Wright was terminated, and Hurley's stock option was cancelled. A refinancing plan was worked out, with financial institutions agreeing to cancel notes totaling $54.7 million in exchange for 5-percent secured notes totaling $16.5 million and 165,000 shares of $5 convertible preferred stock, par value $100 per share.

Churchill had come up with a sharp new car, but it came at a cost. Although the financiers were encouraged by the new product, to protect themselves they had the company pledge virtually all its property and plants as collateral. It was critical that the new car be a success; Studebaker was betting the farm.

1958 advertising tried to give the impression that the Studebakers were all-new, big cars. However, they were merely facelifted 1957s. Left: President Harold Churchill.

A LARK AND A PRAYER

The new car had to be based on the existing body. The most the company could afford was new front and rear sheet metal, so Churchill's choices were few. Since another facelift of the "big" Studebaker would only cause a further drop in sales, he decided to turn his big car into a compact instead. It would be called the Lark.

Design work was completed by March 1958. The new Lark featured distinctive styling, a spacious interior and trim exterior dimensions. At 175 inches in length it was 16 inches shorter than the Rambler Six. Body styles included two- and four-door sedans and a two-door wagon, and a good-looking two-door hardtop. Lark sedans and hardtops featured a generous 108.5-inch wheelbase while station wagons rode a 113-inch chassis. Prices ranged from $1,925 for the Deluxe two-door Lark VI to $2,590 for the Lark VIII two-door wagon. Also debuting were the Lark-based three-passenger Utility Sedan, two-door Panel Wagon, and Econ-O-Miler Taxi.

Lark's standard engine was a 90hp, 169.6-cid flat-head six, with an optional 259-cid V8 offered in 180hp or 195hp versions. *Popular Science* called Lark "a fresh idea," adding: "Sixteen inches shorter than the Rambler, it doesn't have the Rambler's big-car appearance ... the Lark looks more like something from Europe." With the Lark's introduction the company abandoned the full-size car market.

It was an immediate success, and production rapidly increased to meet demand. Many Big Three dealers who wanted to get in on the compact boom became Studebaker franchisees. The company also acquired distribution rights for the Auto Union-DKW line of cars to provide dealers with another product to sell.

The Lark brought Studebaker back from the brink. For 1959 sales climbed to 160,826 cars, 10,909 trucks and 10,588 Mercedes-Benz/Auto Union vehicles vs. 62,146 cars, 10,735 trucks and 6,420 Mercedes-Benz units in 1958. A profit of $28,544,388 was reported and with tax-loss carry-forward credits it was all tax-free, making it the largest net profit in the company's history.

One aspect of the 1958 refinancing/restructuring deal was a requirement that Studebaker diversify into other fields to ensure corporate survival if the auto business failed. Because Curtis-Wright failed to go through with a merger, Studebaker still had more than $100 million in tax-loss carry-forwards. Merger and acquisitions specialist A.M. Sonnabend was hired to find suitable companies for Studebaker to acquire. The first were C.T.L. (Cincinnati Testing Laboratories), a specialty plastics company that produced Titan missile nose cones, and Gering Plastics Inc., producer of plastic compounds.

Competition increased in 1960 when the Chevrolet Corvair, Ford Falcon, Mercury Comet and Chrysler Valiant debuted, causing many Big Three dealers who signed Studebaker franchises in 1959 to drop them now that their own brands offered compacts. Studebaker expanded the Lark range for 1960 with convertible and four-door station wagon models, and introduced new Champ pick-ups with a stylish cab based on Lark sheet metal. Sales held up initially but orders soon began to drop. Sales totaled 133,984 units, down from 182,323 in 1959. Net profits were only $708,850 and the auto division lost money. The company continued to diversify, with Clarke Floor Machines, D.W. Onan and Gravely Tractors joining the growing Studebaker family.

Several board members proposed exiting the car business. Churchill objected and by the end of the year he was replaced as president by Sherwood Egbert, formerly with McCulloch Corporation. Egbert was a hard driver, patrolling offices early morning to late at night, asking questions, ordering changes. He personally spoke with more than 700 Studebaker dealers, soliciting suggestions for improvements. Egbert laid out a four-part plan to restore the company to profitability:

1) Continue and expand the acquisitions program.
2) Strengthen the automotive division's competitive position.
3) Seek a larger share of military business.
4) Create an International Division to sell the company's broad range of products overseas.

For 1961, Lark got a new 112hp Skybolt overhead-valve six and styling changes including a flatter roof and lowered cowl, hood and rear deck. There was a new grille, and Regal and Cruiser models got standard quad headlamps. A Cruiser V8 four-door on the wagon's 113-inch wheelbase debuted. Cruiser offered abundant interior space, a standard 259-cid V8 and

The 1959 Lark (above right and below) and Hawk (above left) used similar front-end styling themes. The new Lark saved Studebaker and provided the highest new profit in the company's history up to that point.

than offset the loss, so the company showed a net profit of $2.535 million for the year. A turnaround appeared imminent. Car sales began to climb, the acquired divisions were profitable, and in the fourth quarter Studebaker-Packard netted a profit of $12.8 million.

Brooks Stevens restyled the Lark for 1962, extending the grille area forward and adding a rich Mercedes-type grille. Longer rear fenders and deck helped increase length by up to 13 inches and all four-door sedans now used the same 113-inch platform as wagons and Cruisers. The sporty Daytona also debuted with standard bucket seats, center console and full carpeting, plus an available four-speed transmission and 225hp, 289-cid V8. Stevens also restyled the Hawk, removing the fins and creating a long, flat roofline to completely change the silhouette and provide more interior room. Called the Gran Turismo Hawk, it was a fast, beautiful tourer.

Egbert announced the new Avanti high-performance sports coupe, with stunning looks and room for four. The fiberglass-bodied Avanti bristled with innovation, offering standard front disc brakes, bucket seats, an aircraft-inspired overhead console and a concealed safety roll bar. A supercharged V8 and four-speed transmission were available.

In 1962 the company was renamed Studebaker Corporation; directors felt including Packard in the corporate name was harming business. Five additional companies were acquired: home appliance maker Franklin Manufacturing; Trans International Airlines, a contract carrier for the military; Schaefer, manufacturer of commercial frozen food and dairy equipment; Domowatt S.P.A., an Italian appliance maker; and Paxton Products, maker of the Paxton supercharger. Although the auto division was still in the red, the company reported a 1962 profit of $2.56 million, which included an operating profit of $489,000. Production of 99,476 cars and trucks in the United States and Canada was up 8 percent over the 92,434 built the prior year, and Mercedes-Benz sales set a new record with 13,300 cars sold. In November, Studebaker

plush interior trim. In March, Chemical Compounds Inc., maker of STP oil treatment, was acquired.

Egbert worked to improve the dealer network, replacing weak dealers with stronger ones; 180 new dealers were signed in the last four months of the year, bringing the total to 2,102 dealers. He also established factory retail outlets in big cities where Studebaker-Packard had few dealerships. For 1961 sales fell to 102,932 units and the company suffered an operating loss of $3.1 million. But selling Gering Plastics Division for a net profit of $5.66 million more

The 1960 Lark (above) was promoted by advertising that listed points of differentiation.

The 1960 Lark (above) was available in six body styles: convertible, hardtop, four-door station wagon, two-door station wagon, four-door sedan, and two-door sedan. Below: The 1960 Hawk.

expanded its import base, acquiring Canadian distribution rights for Mercedes-Benz and DKW.

The reason the automotive division lost money in 1962 was a strike that shut down production for 38 days, strangling the division's comeback. With the exception of the strike months January and February, the first nine months of the year saw dramatic increases in car sales.

The 1963 Lark got a more contemporary look. Brooks Stevens restyled the greenhouse with thin window frames and a flatter roofline and windshield. Three trim levels were offered initially: Regal, Custom and Daytona. The stripped down Standard series appeared mid-year, with prices starting at just $1,935. The new Wagonaire also debuted, featuring a sliding rear roof section so tall items like refrigerators could be carried upright.

Soon, Avanti ran into trouble. First it was production delays that caused impatient buyers to cancel orders;

then, once the problems were fixed and cars were readily available, the company found it had overestimated its sales potential. Unsold Avantis began to pile up.

Egbert wasn't ready to quit. High-performance Avanti R-1 and R-2 engines became options to spur Lark and Hawk sales. Andy Granatelli and a team of drivers took a fleet of Studebakers to the Bonneville Salt Flats, setting 72 new USAC records including an incredible 170.8 mph average in an Avanti with Granatelli at the wheel.

But with the Big Three introducing new intermediates there simply was too much competition.

Above: A front view of the 1960 Lark. Right: The 1963 Hawk.

Studebaker's 1963 sales fell to 64,570 units, a 17-percent decline and far below breakeven. Although volume of $403 million was up $38 million from the prior year, the automotive division lost so much money – exceeding $25 million – the other divisions' combined earnings of more than $11 million failed to offset it and the company suffered an operating loss of $16.9 million. One way or another the problem had to be fixed or the company would simply go broke.

Egbert envisioned a new line of Avanti II cars, two- and four-door sedans based on the Lark chassis with styling inspired by the Avanti coupe. But by then several board members advocated liquidating the auto division and Egbert was unable to continue fighting. The company president had cancer and in November 1963 the board put him on indefinite leave, appointing finance VP Byers Burlingame to take his place.

The banks refused to lend any more money to the auto division unless the corporation agreed to put up its acquired divisions as collateral. The board was unwilling to risk the stockholder's investment, forcing the auto division to pay its own way. Lacking the money to produce the Avanti II or a new Lark proposed by Stevens, all that could be done was another facelift of the existing car. On a shoestring budget Stevens managed to make the 1964 Larks appear almost all-new. If they sold well the division could continue; if not, Studebaker's life as automaker was effectively over.

The GT Hawk and Avanti received only minor updating for 1964 but the Larks featured completely new frontal styling. Three series were offered in six-cylinder and V8 models: Challenger, Commander and Daytona, plus a V8 Cruiser. Unfortunately, within weeks it was clear the new cars weren't selling. There was an 86-day supply in dealers' hands and 3,000 1963 models remained unshipped; production halted for a week to reduce inventories.

than 20,000 units. Hamilton's workforce was increased from 700 to 1,100 people. To streamline production the Hawk, Challenger, Avanti and trucks were all dropped.

Studebaker sold its U.S. foundry, body, engine and final assembly plants and several other buildings for $13 million, which was applied to debt reduction. Its military truck plant was sold to Kaiser Jeep Corporation.

With South Bend's closure, retail sales collapsed, declining to 35,373 in the United States and Canada for 1964, versus 73,277 the prior year. Most were cars produced in South Bend before the end of 1963. However, although sales fell to $261 million, plummeting more than $140 million, Studebaker earned $8 million, its first significant profit since 1959. Management investigated importing a low-priced foreign car for its dealers to sell; one possibility was Toyota, a virtually unknown brand.

Studebaker's 325 Canadian dealers had retailed 7,658 cars in 1964 while the 1,700 U.S. dealers sold 27,715. Exceeding the 20,000-car breakeven in 1965 now seemed a reasonable expectation. Because South

By December 1963 the company was bleeding to death. On Dec. 7, the board reached a decision to shut down Studebaker's South Bend plant and transfer all car production to the company's plant in Hamilton, Ontario. Burlingame explained: "The basic difficulty in South Bend was insufficient volume of sales. Our facilities there were such that there was no way to reduce our costs so that a profit could be made upon such volume. The Canadian plant ... can be operated at a profit on much lower volume. Therefore we have decided to live with the sales we have rather than to continue to hope they will improve."

The company took a special charge of $64 million to cover anticipated losses on disposal of plants, property, tools and inventory, bringing the total loss for 1963 to more than $80 million. By year's end Studebaker's net worth had shrunk to $36.7 million.

Hamilton could produce upwards of 36,000 cars annually. Although breakeven was once 7,000 cars, after South Bend closed the plant carried the overhead for the entire sales division, raising breakeven to more

Top: The 1963 Studebaker Avanti would go on to become collectible. Above: Brooks Stevens crafted a new front-end panel that extended the grille forward to eliminate the Lark's stubby appearance. New rear fenders were longer than before, and wheelbases were increased.

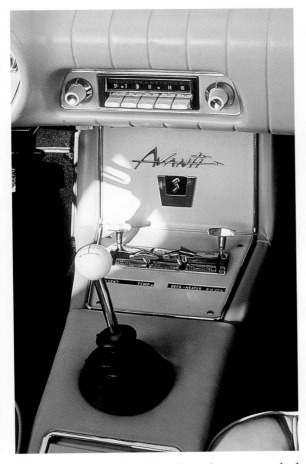

The Avanti of 1963 was special in many ways beside exterior styling. The high-performance Studebaker shown here is a V8, four-speed version, with comfortable back seats and ample appointments for the driver.

Bend no longer produced engines, the company had to find another source. McKinnon Industries of St. Catherine's, Ontario, a GM subsidiary, agreed to supply Chevy six and V8 engines. Production of the 1965 cars began in August 1964 with introduction scheduled for October. With no styling changes to speak of, the company boasted its cars offered the most standard equipment in their class. The line-up included 10 models: Commander two- and four-door sedans and a wagon, plus a Cruiser four-door, all offering six-cylinder or V8 engines. The Daytona (V8 only) offered a two-door Sport sedan and a four-door wagon; no convertibles or hardtops were offered. In all, just 19,435 1965 Studebakers were built. The company

reported total sales of $192 million, down $69 million from prior year, but earned a $10.7 million profit. That February the Mercedes-Benz distribution rights were sold to Daimler-Benz.

Trade rules allowed home market producers to import cars into Canada duty-free, so auto division president Gordon Grundy tried to increase income by making a deal with Volkswagen to import VWs and

sell them to Volkswagen Canada for a slightly lower price, with Studebaker earning a $150 profit on each. His attempts to get distribution rights to Toyota or Datsun cars came to nothing.

For 1966 a Dearborn, Mich., design firm, Marcks, Hazelquist and Powers (MHP), was hired to restyle the cars. Bob Marcks, a talented ex-Loewy designer, freshened up the frontal appearance with a handsome new grille, dual headlamps to replace the quads, and lower bodyside moldings. To upgrade the car's image Marcks specified rich interior fabrics and elegant colors and trim of the type usually seen in luxury cars. The line-up included Commander two and four-door sedans, a Wagonaire, Daytona two-door sedan and Cruiser four-door, each offering six or V8 power. Prices began as low as $2,060.

As good-looking as the new cars were, management decided to close out the business. On March 4 they announced that production would end the following day. Only 2,045 cars had been produced during calendar 1966, an annual rate equal to just 12,000 units per year. Management said the auto division closure was due to "heavy and irreversible losses," though Grundy claimed his division was operating profitably at the time. Facts tend to support management's statement: Although the breakeven point was 20,000 units (about 10 cars per year for each of Studebaker's 2,000 U.S. and Canadian dealers) sales didn't reach that in 1965,

Top: The 1964 Studebaker GT Hawk. Above: Bob Marcks of Marcks, Hazelquist and Powers designed this 1967 prototype, a hint of what may have been.

and the production rate in early 1966 was running well below 20,000 cars annually.

Meanwhile, MHP had nearly completed designing the 1967 Studebakers, with minor changes that greatly improved the styling. Using a 1966 car MHP mocked-up a 1967 model, with thick side moldings and a rear bumper raised to just below the decklid for a sleeker look. A new grille featured two panels inside a larger rectangle. The handsome styling compared well with competitors.

Marcks also created proposals for designs to carry Studebaker to 1970 and beyond. A complete redesign was out of the question, so MHP focused on restyling the existing car. One concept was a sedan with Hawk styling themes; another featured a sloping hood and twin grilles like the 1953 models. A gold four-door sedan represented what Studebaker might look like in 1970.

Naturally, the corporation continued on despite the car division shutdown. Management considered the remaining divisions a foundation to grow on. The company became America's largest producer of tire studs

In 1973 – the 10th anniversary of South Bend's closing – Studebaker-Worthington sales exceeded $1 billion. Onan sales alone were more than $100 million, STP sales were $87 million, Clarke-Gravely $58 million and Schaeffer just under $10 million. If Studebaker had remained independent it would have had annual sales of well over $250 million.

Studebaker-Worthington was acquired by McGraw-Edison in 1979, and a few years afterward McGraw-Edison was absorbed by Cooper Industries. With no attachment to any particular product the Studebaker name faded away. But it had long ceased to be the same company. Its old slogan "Always Give The Customer More Than You Promise" was out of date. Studebaker-Worthington had become a conglomerate that boasted mainly about how much money it made.

Farewell, Studebaker. Although it's sad to lose so great an automaker, you left behind a heritage of great cars and trucks, a rich legacy that can never fade away. ▲Q

Above: The 1966 Cruiser. Below right: A rare glimpse of the Avanti II sedan that Sherwood Egbert wanted the company to produce. It wasn't to be.

for snow tires, and acquired Big Four Industries, maker of tire-studding guns and tire-changing equipment.

Sales dropped again in 1966, to $172 million but net income rose to $16.4 million. Other companies became interested in Studebaker; its remaining tax-loss carry-forwards making it a good prospect for merger. The company held talks with Wagner Electric Corporation, meanwhile selling two under-performing divisions, Cincinnati Testing Laboratories and Franklin Appliance, which by then were barely profitable.

Studebaker, Wagner Electric and Worthington Industries came together in 1967 to form Studebaker-Worthington Inc. It brought together Studebaker's profitable divisions: Clarke Floor Machines, Gravely Tractors, Schaefer, Chemical Compounds (which eventually was renamed STP Corp.) and Onan, with Wagner Electric's automotive electrical and brake businesses and Worthington's diverse holdings in construction equipment, valve and power-generation businesses. The new corporation's annual sales revenue for 1967 exceeded $650 million.

KEEPERS OF THE FLAME

Studebaker National Museum

More than 40 years have passed since the last Studebaker was built, yet the Studebaker legacy remains evident in South Bend, Ind. The Studebaker National Museum lies just a few hundred yards from the former Studebaker plant. Clement Studebaker's grand mansion, Tippecanoe Place, is now one of the city's fine dining establishments. South Bend's YMCA and Memorial Hospital were founded with Studebaker money, and vestiges of the city's largest employer abound. The museum opened a new facility in October 2005, but its roots lie with company founder Clement Studebaker more than a century before.

BY ANDREW BECKMAN

23

On Feb. 16, 1852, a new business opened at the corner of Michigan and Jefferson streets in downtown South Bend. The enterprise was called H & C Studebaker; services offered were blacksmithing and wagon-making. Proprietors Henry and Clement Studebaker were the eldest of John and Rebecca Studebaker's five sons. The brothers learned the blacksmithing and wagon-making trades at their father's side and saw opportunity in the growing community located on the south bend of the St. Joseph River.

H & C Studebaker's first customer needed a horse shod; the bill totaled 25 cents. The first year saw the brothers spend far more time at the forge than building

STUDEBAKER BROTHERS' CARRIAGE AND WAGON FACTORY, SOUTH BEND, IND.

wagons. Total wagon output for 1852 was two units.

Despite these modest beginnings, the company quickly grew. John M. Studebaker joined the business in 1857, buying out Henry Studebaker's stake in the firm. Peter Studebaker came aboard in 1863 to head up the sales department. His agreement with brother Clement stated: "I, Peter Studebaker, agree to sell all wagons my brother Clement can make." Clement countersigned, "I, Clement Studebaker, agree to make all the wagons my brother Peter can sell." Jacob Studebaker signed on following the completion of his coursework at the University of Notre Dame in 1868. He was placed in charge of the Carriage Department, and the company was rechristened the Studebaker Brothers Manufacturing Company. By the 1880s, the company was the world's largest builder of wagons and buggies.

Left: The Studebaker Brothers (left to right): Henry, Jacob, Clement, Peter, John M. Above: In the Studebaker National Museum's collection is this carriage President Abraham Lincoln took to Ford's Theatre the night he was assasinated.

Above: A circa 1940s image of Studebaker Light Six serial number 1,000,001. It currently shows 19 miles on the odometer. Right: A young couple pose with their 1931 President Four Season Roadster in front of the "giant" President located at the Studebaker Proving Ground from 1930-1936.

BEGINNING THE COLLECTION

It was at this time that Clement Studebaker began acquiring vehicles for the Studebaker Bros. collection. In the early 1820s, the U. S. government commissioned John Curlet of Baltimore, Md., to construct a carriage for the Marquis de Lafayette's 1824 tour of the United States. Conventional wisdom of the day held that any fine carriage must come from Europe. But, given that Lafayette's tour was in celebration of his service to the American Revolution, a European carriage simply would not do. The Lafayette carriage is one of the earliest examples of fine carriage making in the United States. Mr. Studebaker purchased the carriage in 1887, and it remains the oldest vehicle in the Studebaker collection.

In August 1890, Clement Studebaker acquired the carriage that President Abraham Lincoln took to Ford's

Theatre the night of his assassination. The Lincoln carriage was manufactured by the Wood Brothers of New York and presented to President Lincoln shortly after his second inauguration by a group of New York citizens. Following the assassination, the carriage was sold to a Dr. F.B. Brewer of New York. Mr. Studebaker sought and obtained the Lincoln family's blessing before pur-

chasing the carriage, and it joined the Lafayette carriage on display at Studebaker's Chicago Repository.

The Lincoln carriage recently returned from a year-long conservation treatment at the hands of Brian Howard Associates of Carlisle, Penn. This work was undertaken as part of a "Save America's Treasures" grant the museum received in 2005 to conserve eight vehicles.

Conservator Howard stabilized all at-risk areas on the carriage and exposed areas of original finishes and striping. The carriage's original livery was a dark green body with black trim and delicate striping on the wheels and suspension. Additionally, each door carried President Lincoln's monogram. Howard's work uncovered the body's original hue and revealed Lincoln's monogram for the first time in more than a century.

The company also made a conscious effort to acquire and/or retain vehicles of its own manufacture. Studebaker-built carriages belonging to presidents Harrison, McKinley and Grant were purchased in the

Left: The Bendix "SWC," the only automobile ever produced by Bendix Aviation. Right: The "No. 6" 1928 Commander roadster is shown on a publicity tour in late 1928.

early 1900s. Studebaker's last buggy and Farm Wagon were built in 1919 and 1920, respectively, and immediately placed in the collection.

The Studebaker Corporation's departure from horsedrawn production kicked off a massive overhaul of the company's South Bend plant. Although Studebaker had marketed automobiles since 1902, nearly all automobile production took place at its Detroit factories. However, automobiles were now Studebaker's sole product and would be built in South Bend. Studebaker's new Albert Kahn-designed Light Six automobile plant debuted with much fanfare in 1920. Light Six serial number 1,000,001 was placed in the company collection and today registers but 19 miles on the odometer.

A 1924 Light Six is a more recent addition to the collection. It carries custom coachwork by the Shanghai Horse Bazaar and Automobile Company of Shanghai, China. In 1916, Studebaker commissioned Coy Goodrich to serve as the plant manager and sales liaison with the Shanghai Horse Bazaar Co. Shanghai

Horse Bazaar craftsmen were capable of creating very attractive designs with the utmost attention to detail. Goodrich oversaw the plant until he returned to the United States in 1923.

Shortly after his return, Goodrich arranged to have a custom-built 1923 Studebaker coupe body shipped to him in San Francisco. This body was one of five made in handcrafted aluminum and is finished in dark blue. The interior is trimmed in teak with dark blue mohair upholstery. Upon its arrival in the United States, Goodrich had the body mated to a 1924 Light Six chassis. The car was driven regularly until 1937 and remained in the Goodrich family until it was presented to the Studebaker National Museum by Coy Goodrich's son, George, in 2004.

Another highlight of the museum collection is a pair of record-setting Commanders that hail from the original Studebaker collection. In the fall of 1928, a trio of Commanders was dispatched to a racetrack in Atlantic City, N.J., with orders to complete 25,000 miles as quickly as possible. For 15 days and nights,

the Commanders lapped the dilapidated board track, stopping only to replenish fluids, change tires and switch drivers. The "No. 6" Commander roadster completed its 25,000 miles first, doing so in just under 23,000 minutes.

Approximately one year earlier, David Abbot "Ab" Jenkins piloted a 1927 Commander sedan from New York City to San Francisco in 77 hours, 40 minutes, covering 3,302 miles in the process. Jenkins' journey nearly ended in disaster when an unmarked curve near Lincoln, Neb., led to an unplanned detour through a farmer's field. Upon exiting the roadway, the Commander went airborne for nearly 30 feet. The resulting damage was serious but not insurmountable as Jenkins was able to resume his journey and break the record. The car still exhibits evidence of Jenkins' mishap; a front fender and the body mounts show visible trauma, and areas of mud and straw can be found in the deep recesses of the undercarriage. It should be noted the record Jenkins broke was his own, set one year earlier in a 1926 Studebaker Big Six.

Above: The AM General Atrium and Body Drop display. The LARK letters are from South Bend's Newman & Altman dealership. Below: A 1932 President convertible coupe.

THE MISSION

The Studebaker National Museum's mission not only encompasses the products and history of the Studebaker Corporation but also of other South Bend area businesses and industries. The Steel Wheel Corporation may be an unfamiliar name, but many are well acquainted with the products of South Bend-based Bendix Aviation. The Steel Wheel Corporation was a paper company created by Bendix, which, under this guise, produced one automobile in 1934. This car is naturally equipped with nearly every automotive product Bendix made but carries "SWC" badging as Vincent Bendix did not want his biggest customers to believe he was entering into the automobile business. The Bendix car was placed on loan to the museum in 1977 and was formally gifted to the museum by the Honeywell Corporation in 2005.

The Studebaker Corporation and the Packard Motor Car Company's 1954 merger did little to help either firm but did result in several Packard vehicles and artifacts entering the collection. The Packard Predictor was spared the fate of many show cars and prototypes following its 1956 auto show tour and spent several years under a tarpaulin at the Studebaker Proving Ground garage. The Predictor received a restoration by Lavine Restorations of Nappanee, Ind., in the late 1980s and resides in the museum's upper level gallery.

On Dec. 9, 1963, the Studebaker Corporation announced that it was closing the South Bend plant, and all remaining production would be consolidated at the company's Hamilton, Ontario, facility. The last regular production South Bend-built Studebaker was completed on December 20, 1963. Like the first Light Six built 43 years earlier, this Bordeaux Red Daytona Hardtop was immediately placed in the company collection.

Across the aisle from the Daytona sits the last Studebaker ever built. Some confusion exists as to the exact production date of this 1966 Cruiser, as company documents list both March 16 and March 17, 1966. Studebaker National Museum Life Trustee and former

Above: Ab Jenkins's mount for his 1927 coast-to-coast dash. Right: The 1961 Hawk. Its "Flamingo" finish was exclusive to 1961 Hawks and Lark covertibles.

Studebaker of Canada Director of Advertising Stu Chapman explains that the car was completed on March 16 and left at the end of line, as the media was scheduled to arrive shortly after 8:00 the following morning. The car officially exited the line on the March 17 after having been completed by workers the day before.

The last Studebaker did not immediately enter the collection, as it was placed in service and driven by company executives. It entered the collection two years later, having logged 17,000 miles and sporting snow tires. The Cruiser received a cosmetic restoration in 1999-2000 by Studebaker National Museum volunteers. During the project several areas were discovered where Studebaker workers had "personalized" the car. Names and initials were found etched in the firewall, and "Last Panel Assembled by R B" is written on the underside of the instrument panel.

When the Studebaker Corporation ceased automobile production in March 1966, the 37-unit collection and company archives were given to the city of South Bend. The agreement stipulated that the city provide a "suitable home" to house and display the vehicles. The collection had several different homes during the next 40 years, including the former Studebaker Administration Building and South Bend's Century Center convention center.

The museum moved into the former Freeman-Spicer Studebaker dealership in 1982. This building dated to 1916 and was originally built as a Studebaker-owned retail outlet and service center. Although the Freeman-Spicer building served gallantly as the museum's home for the next 23 years, increasing structural and environmental limitations precluded its use much beyond the year 2000. In 2003, planning began in earnest for a brand-new 55,000-square-foot facility in partnership with the city of South Bend. The new Studebaker National Museum would be located adjacent to the Center for History, St. Joseph County's history museum, creating a unique "museum campus" setting.

VISITING THE MUSEUM

On Oct. 28, 2005, the Studebaker National Museum opened its new building. Nine main exhibit areas on three levels begin with the Studebaker family's arrival from Germany in 1736, concluding with the Studebaker's lasting legacy in the present day. More than 70 vehicles are on interpreted display with an additional 30 vehicles in visible storage on the museum's lower level. In "Visible Storage," vehicles not currently on exhibit are housed in two-tiered racking and can be seen every day by museum-goers. Galleries and collection storage areas are temperature and humidity controlled.

The lower level is also home to the museum's military collection. H & C Studebaker's first military contract came in 1857 to supply wagons for the Mormon War in Utah. The Studebaker shop also supplied wagons to the Union Army during the Civil War, and produced military vehicles and equipment for every armed conflict through the Vietnam War. Studebaker-built U.S. Army ambulances and water carts from World War I are on display, as is a World War II Weasel and Wright Cyclone R-1820 B17 bomber engine. When the Studebaker Corporation closed the South Bend plant in December 1963, Kaiser-Jeep acquired Studebaker's military contracts and facilities in South Bend. Kaiser-Jeep evolved into AM General, which produces Hummer H2s in

Just one exquisite example to be found in the Carmichael Bullet Nose Gallery.

neighboring Mishawaka, Ind.

Visitors to the museum enter the exhibit galleries via the AM General Atrium. This space was inspired by images of Studebaker building no. 78, which featured an open high-bay area and peaked-roof skylight. The atrium showcases the museum's "Body Drop" display and is also a popular location for special events and facility rentals. Up to 120 people can be seated for dinner events. The far end of the AM General Atrium leads to the Carmichael Bullet Nose Gallery, which features a revolving turntable and street-level showroom windows.

In addition to the vehicle collection, the museum boasts more than 4,000 items in its small artifacts collection. This collection includes a large number of employee-related items such as service pins, uniforms and identification badges as well as product-related artifacts.

Of the entire small artifact collection, one particular hubcap draws the most comments. No ordinary hubcap, it measures over two feet in diameter and is a relic of Studebaker's grandest automobile advertisement. In late 1930, Studebaker's Experimental Body Division built a 40-foot-long wooden replica of a 1931

President Four Season Roadster. It sat near the main gate of the Studebaker Proving Ground and was a popular attraction for VIPs and tourists. However, by 1936 the car was badly weathered and no longer resembled current Studebaker automobiles. Studebaker officials decided that it was time for the giant roadster to go. That spring, the hubcaps were removed, the rumble seat was opened and a front fender was doused in gasoline. A torch was applied, and in 30 minutes the car was reduced to ashes.

The whereabouts of the five hubcaps remained unknown until one walked in the front door in the mid-1990s. Another was acquired when museum staff received a phone message that simply read, "Studebaker hubcap." The other three caps remain at large.

One of the most frequently asked questions is if the museum has a "bullet nose" on display. Indeed, a 1950 Commander Starlight Coupe can be found in the museum's upper level gallery. Other iconic Studebaker automobiles such as a 1953 Starliner hardtop and a 1934 Commander Land Cruiser are also on display in the upper level gallery. The museum collection also features a number of Studebaker commercial vehicles including a 1937 Coupe Express, a 1947 M5 pickup, and a recently acquired 1949 2R5 pickup.

The upper level gallery is also home to the museum's special exhibit area which rotates every six to nine months. Previous exhibits have featured alternative fuel vehicles, muscle cars and Indiana-built automobiles. Upcoming exhibits will showcase British sports cars, pickup trucks and Harley-Davidson motorcycles.

The Studebaker National Museum would not exist today if it were not for the dedicated efforts of the Studebaker Drivers Club, Antique Studebaker Club and the Avanti Owners Association International. These organizations have made significant contributions to the museum in both finances and collections.

Above: Studebaker National Museum Archives. Left: The Design Studio display features artwork and artifacts from Raymond Loewy's Studebaker design chief Robert Bourke.

To honor the clubs' years of support, the museum features a "Club Room" on the upper level. Each club provided materials and images for the room, and it is also home to several club member memorials.

In June 2007, the museum served as host for the Studebaker Drivers Club 43rd International Meet. The Studebaker Drivers Club was joined by the Antique Studebaker Club, Avanti Owners Association International and the Packard Club for the week-long event. More than 1,000 Studebakers, Packards and Avantis visited South Bend that week, and more than 3,000 people registered for meet activities. Many experienced the new museum for the first time at the meet's Welcome Night. Museum trustees welcomed meet-goers to an ice cream social that evening, dishing out more than 1,000 scoops of ice cream.

THE ARCHIVES

The Studebaker National Museum Archives holds the surviving archives of the Studebaker Corporation and the Packard Motor Car Company. The archives were included in the Studebaker Corporation's donation to South Bend in 1966. Syracuse University expressed interest in the archives, and the 70-plus tons of material was shipped to New York later that year. The archives spent the next decade at Syracuse before returning to Sound Bend in 1977. Today, the archives' primary holdings include an image collection with more than 50,000 images, company publications, sales literature and dealer and production records. The largest and most frequently

Above: South Bend's last Studebaker, a 1964 Daytona hardtop. Below: Lapping the former Studebaker test track at the 2007 Studebaker Drivers Club International Meet.

requested collection is of Studebaker and Packard engineering drawings. These drawings date to the teens and encompass parts large and small. Trim clip and gaskets are covered on a normal sheet of paper, while body layout drawings and engine blocks are rendered actual size and stretch for several yards.

Like the museum's vehicle collection, the archives have had several homes since their return to South Bend. Its most recent home was located several miles from the museum campus.

In tandem with the planning for the new museum building, Studebaker National Museum Trustees began looking for a new location for the archives. In 2005, the Indiana Department of Transportation greenlighted a federally funded project to renovate a 19th century commercial building into the new Studebaker National Museum Archives. The building, previously occupied by a grocery store and several taverns, had the added benefit of being located just across the street from the museum campus. Plans called for the building to be completely gutted and rebuilt from within to handle the massive amount of archival material. The project created a "building within a building" while leaving the exterior essentially unchanged.

In October 2007, the Studebaker National Museum Archives opened its new facility. The archives feature a public reading room, regular hours of operation as well as climate-controlled stacks and storage areas.

To ask people what brings them to the Studebaker National Museum elicits many different answers. Visitors from the surrounding area often mention that a relative worked for Studebaker. Others are Studebaker owners; it is not uncommon to see a Studebaker or two in the parking lot during summer months. One couple stated that they had their first date in a Studebaker and hoped that that model was on display.

The Studebaker brothers' motto was, "Always Give More Than You Promise." The brothers' hard work and foresight established a lasting legacy into the 21st century. They are still giving more than they promised. AQ

BERND ROSEMEYER

Auto Union's Superstar

F ew others than Bernd Rosemeyer, before or since, in the short time allotted him, have made a larger impact on Grand Prix racing. And those who never witnessed his magic behind the wheel still study his all too brief career.

BY L. SPENCER RIGGS

33

On a warm summer evening in 1926, Wilhelm Rosemeyer was relaxing in his modest home. He wondered aloud to his wife, Louise, why their 16-year-old son was so late arriving home. Frau Rosemeyer may have made some excuse for the absence of her impetuous boy, whom she was reluctantly giving up to young manhood.

Then came a rapping at the door. Frau Rosemeyer opened it and found a policeman standing there. "Do you have a son named Bernd?" the gruff officer inquired. Frau Rosemeyer replied that she did. At that instant, the policeman pulled a slightly built, blond youth from the shadows. Even before the lad was visible in the light from inside the house, his mother recognized the contagious grin.

Asked what he had done, Bernd, still smiling, gestured for the officer to explain. "No man may ride down the street of Lingen, Germany, doing a handstand on the handlebars of a motorcycle," the officer growled. "We impounded his bike. Next time, we will impound him, too!" The officer turned to leave, but an afterthought occurred to him. "He appears to have no fear at all," he remarked.

Top: The Auto Union team in the paddock at the 1936 Italian Grand Prix. The rear-engine C-type cars, from left to right, were piloted by: Ernst von Delius, Achille Varzi, Bernd Rosemeyer and Hans Stuck. Above: Rosemeyer in his famous 16-cylinder Auto Union during practice at the Nürburgring in 1936. The rear-engine machine with swing axles on the rear was a real handful.

In the years to come, that statement would be repeated many times.

Bernhard "Bernd" Rosemeyer was born Oct. 14, 1909, in Lingen. His father owned a garage, and from childhood Bernd was surrounded by engines.

Not long after his run-in with the police, young Rosemeyer, inspired by stories he read about the exploits of Rudi Caracciola, Otto Merz, Tazio Nuvolari and Achille Varzi, expressed his desire to become a motorcycle racer. Because his parents were completely against the idea, the lad kept his ultimate goal secret. His greatest desire was to become a Grand Prix driver – champion of Germany, maybe even Europe. His dream never died, and with his happy-go-lucky wit and charm, no one could ever say no to Bernd for long.

In 1930, he started racing motorcycles on grass tracks. Because part of negotiating such slippery courses consisted of controlling the art of sliding, many feel it was here that Rosemeyer learned his spectacular technique that would amaze his rivals and

Above: Surrounded by admiring fans, Rosemeyer poses behind the wheel of his Auto Union in 1936. That year, he was European and German Road Racing Champion.

admirers in years to come. By 1932, he had moved up to road racing with a BMW cycle. This was quickly followed by a 500cc NSU full-racing machine, which he entered in his first professional race at Hanover. The factory team manager for NSU was so impressed that he signed Rosemeyer to a contract. In 1933, he rewarded NSU by winning six major events for them.

By 1934 Rosemeyer was an established member of the DKW factory motorcycle racing team. He had already won more than his share of events. Since DKW was part of the combine that formed Auto Union, he had a good chance to make his talents known to company officials.

During that same year, during a motorcycle event at the Nürburgring, the transition from two wheels to four – from motorcycle to automobile – took shape.

Rosemeyer won the event with a flashy, masterful display of riding. But more important, the cycle event was a preliminary for the Eifel Grand Prix. Rosemeyer fell in love with the powerful 16-cylinder rear-engine Auto Union designed by Dr. Ferdinand Porsche and driven by Hans Stuck. He soon put motorcycle racing behind him, investing all his energy in convincing Auto Union's team manager Willie Walb of his capabilities.

A hard-bitten former driver, Walb was a tough taskmaster who had the final say about "AU's" driver assignments. The powerful Auto Union GP car, sprung by rear swing-axles and extreme forward driver placement, was a handful to drive. Walb favored sure-handed, experienced drivers like Stuck. He was not interested in the little wild man. "A Grand Prix team is no place for you," Walb scoffed. "Stick to something

you can jump off of after you lose control."

As Walb was about to learn, saying no to Rosemeyer's challenges, on or off the track, could be a tricky bit. The aspiring champion left messages for the team manager everywhere. He wanted a test drive as soon as possible. Walb put him off until the season was over.

Then, on a cool October morning at the Nürburgring, Rosemeyer showed up for his test drive – wearing a suit and tie. Asked why he wasn't in coveralls, as Walb had instructed, Rosemeyer replied: "This is a very important day in my life, so I thought I'd dress for it."

Walb, already disgruntled, sent him off for some slow laps. "Take it easy," Walb admonished. "This is no toy!" After a lap or two to warm the oil and feel out the machine, Rosemeyer got down to business. Each succeeding lap was faster, until Walb could not believe his stopwatch. After a few more laps, he had seen enough. He ordered the mechanics to flag Rosemeyer in before he killed himself.

They waited – and waited – but as the sweep hand of Walb's watch went five, 10, 15 seconds past the expected time for the Auto Union to thunder into sight, there was no car, no Rosemeyer. For that matter, there was no sound, no indication that a car was even out there on the vast circuit. At last, Rosemeyer's car came into sight, moving slowly toward the pits. Walb let out a string of curses when he saw grass and weeds wound about its suspension and mud splashed over the once shiny, silver bodywork. Obviously, Rosemeyer had lost control and left the track.

He was done as far as Walb was concerned. It was back to the cycles for Rosemeyer and the devil take him! The manager unleashed a torrent of abuses on the young driver, but Rosemeyer only smiled. "Imagine! She took me for a walk," Rosemeyer grinned. "Now, I shall take her for one."

Before Walb and the stunned mechanics could stop him, Rosemeyer smoked the tires out of the pits, the irate manager chasing after him with murder in his eyes. On the following lap, Rosemeyer nearly equaled the lap record. When he returned to the pits, Walb admitted his hastiness of judgment and promptly contracted Rosemeyer to race.

His dream beginning to come to life, Rosemeyer eagerly awaited the 1935 season. But Walb refused to assign him a car. The Tunis and Tripoli events passed, and the Avusrennen in Berlin loomed on the horizon. Walb pronounced the Avus too fast and dangerous for a new driver. "I won't need you for this race, either," the manager flatly told the neophyte chauffeur.

Realizing that an argument would only make him look worse in Walb's eyes, Rosemeyer returned to his tactic of note writing. He wrote notes on Walb's desk calendar. He tucked one into the manager's gloves and another into his coat pocket. One materialized above

Left: Rudi Caracciola was a top-notch Grand Prix ace when Rosemeyer arrived on the scene. Young Rosemeyer's raw talent was quite a shock to the master Mercedes driver. Their epic duels are the stuff of legend. Above: Rosemeyer and his rear-engine Auto Union round the Karussel Curve in his winning drive in the 1936 German Grand Prix at the Nürburgring. Note the young people lining the fence to watch their hero ply his trade.

the headline on his morning paper. He even managed to scribble one on Walb's paycheck. "Why is Rosemeyer not driving yet?" read one note. "Where is the car for Rosemeyer?" asked another. "Will Rosemeyer drive on the Avus?" And so it went.

At one point, Walb was about to explode. But he was nearly ready to give in when the audacious prankster almost overplayed his hand. Seated in a restaurant with friends, Walb unfolded his napkin to find yet another message: "Rosemeyer will drive on the Avis!" Walb looked up just in time to see Rosemeyer approaching – dressed as a waiter. The team manager scribbled "Ja" across the note and handed it to the "waiter."

At Avus, which at this juncture consisted of two six-mile sections of autobahn-like highway connected by two slow turns, Rosemeyer practiced at nearly

153 mph. This was the third-fastest time of the meet. During the opening laps, he ran a strong second, but a blown tire ended his chances of a high finish. Yet it was enough to give the veterans plenty to think about.

A few weeks later, in the Eifelrennen held at the Nürburgring, Rosemeyer showed what he was made of. Entered only as insurance and told to bide his time, the youngster surprised Walb by following orders, running well off the pace in fifth. However, his Auto Union teammates Varzi and Stuck fell by the wayside; Paul Peitsch was too far back to challenge the leading Mercedes trio of Manfred von Brauchitsch, Caracciola and Luigi Fagioli, so Walb gave Rosemeyer the go sign. Within only a few miles he flogged his thundering Auto Union past Louis Chiron's Alfa and Fagioli's Mercedes, setting his sights on second-place

Above left: Rosemeyer in third position at the 1937 German Grand Prix in Nürburgring. Above right: In the same contest, Hermann Lang leads Caracciola, Rosemeyer and H.P. Muller in the early part of the race. Rosemeyer was trying for his fourth straight victory over the treacherous "Ring." However, Caracciola was the winner this time.

Caracciola. "He landed on me like a panther, without warning," Caracciola later remarked. Caracciola was amazed not only by Rosemeyer's speed but also his technique. He had never seen anyone but Nuvolari slide a Grand Prix car though a turn at a full-lock, 90-degree angle. Not even Stuck would attempt such a maneuver in the tail-heavy 375-horsepower Auto Union, a machine quite unsuited to such endeavors. Rosemeyer drove as if the Nürburgring was an American dirt track, not the most demanding road course in the world.

Out front, in an attempt to escape the torrid Caracciola-Rosemeyer duel behind him, Brauchitsch blew his engine. Rosemeyer, hampered by shattered goggles – likely from a rock thrown up by his own front wheels as they left the forest road in the turns – forced the juddering, fishtailing Auto Union around Caracciola and into the lead as they roared by the main grandstand. Caracciola succeeded in closing the gap, but he could not get around the youngster.

Finally, with just one lap to go, Caracciola saw an opportunity. On one of the little switchbacks just before Dottinger-Hohe, the rise heading toward the finishing straight, Rosemeyer shifted into fifth gear a split second too soon. His engine had developed a misfire as well. On that final circuit, the veteran stalked the youngster, waiting for Rosemeyer to make the same mistake again. When he did, Caracciola stayed in fourth a heartbeat longer, slammed his accelerator to the floor and flashed past. He finished less than two seconds ahead of his new rival.

At a banquet that evening, the sensational per-formance of young Rosemeyer dominated all con-versation, and Caracciola let his feelings take over. Watching Rosemeyer from across the room, seeing how sure of himself he looked, the older ace decided to shake up this new upstart. "Well done, my dear fel-low," Caracciola said to Rosemeyer. "But in future, just don't drive around the circuit. Use your head." Then he removed a swizzle stick from his drink and shoved it into Rosemeyer's hand. "You might practice shifting gears with this," the veteran said.

Caught off guard, Rosemeyer was stunned by the champion's words. He tucked the swizzle stick into his lapel, where he would wear it for nearly two years. If anything, the incident fueled Rosemeyer's resolve even more. Caracciola had not seen the last of him.

On July 28, 1935, during the Coppa Acerbo at Pescara, Italy, Rosemeyer, hampered by brake prob-lems, went off the road while dueling with Nuvolari for the lead. He quickly returned to the course. But on the eighth lap, his brakes locked. He rocketed off the road, flattened a kilometer stone, hurtled a ditch, and miraculously passed between a telegraph pole and a house. Two blown rear tires and a long, slow trip to the pits dropped him well behind the field. At this point, most drivers would have given up, but with unbeliev-able tenacity, Rosemeyer fought his way back through the field, finishing second only to Varzi.

Following the race, Dr. Porsche went out to the spot where Rosemeyer had left the road. He measured the

Scenes from the Donington Grand Prix in Great Britain. Above: Rosemeyer during his tremendous 1937 bid smokes the tires of his C-Type as he drifts through a bend. It would be Rosemeyer's last victory.

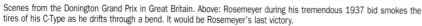

distance between the pole and the house and discovered the gap was about two inches wider than the Auto Union at its widest point. "Mentally, I shook hands with Rosemeyer," Porsche said.

He followed this up with a third-place finish behind Caracciola and Fagioli in the Swiss Grand Prix at Bern.

On Sept. 29, the Czech Grand Prix at Brno, the last big event of the season, lured everyone but the Mercedes team to the huge, rough course. Having won six events, Caracciola had already clinched the German and European road-racing titles. So Mercedes stayed home. On this day, the inevitable happened. After a thrilling early duel with Nuvolari, Rosemeyer defeated the Italian master by six minutes for his first Grand Prix victory.

The first person to congratulate Rosemeyer was Elly Beinhorn, a slim, sunburned young woman who was well known throughout Europe as a long-distance aviatrix. As she stepped close to put the winner's wreath around his neck, Rosemeyer couldn't take his eyes off her. In less than a year they would be married.

Despite his loss, Nuvolari was the first driver to congratulate Rosemeyer. "I am the world's worst loser," Nuvolari confided to a friend. "But it is difficult to deny a talent like his – especially when watching it

from a trailing position."

One does not always win a first race, a wife and a life-long friend all in the same day.

Not only did Nuvolari and Rosemeyer have great respect for one another, but their driving styles had much in common. Both drivers broke all the rules: skidding, sliding, bouncing off curbs, doing whatever was necessary to gain the advantage. Their reckless tactics and flamboyant styles, together with their accessibility to the fans, permanently endeared them to the public.

While Caracciola looked forward to the 1936 season, he soon discovered that some of the fans, especially the younger ones, were being pried away by Rosemeyer. In just a few races, the wisecracking interloper had become Caracciola's archrival.

The Auto Union team was now under the direction of Dr. Karl Feuereissen. Under a much lighter yoke than Walb's, Rosemeyer began to combine his uncanny talents with his head.

At Monaco, on a wet, oily track, Rosemeyer struggled with his Auto Union, while Nuvolari and Caracciola contested the lead. Only a few laps into the race, Rosemeyer crashed into a bridge parapet. Smiling, he arrived at his pit carrying a stone vase that

had toppled from the bridge. "The only cup I'm taking home today," he quipped.

At Tripoli, Rosemeyer was leading when his car caught fire. At Tunis, his machine burst into flames again, causing a horrifying crash. How he walked away unscathed from the twisted, burned-out wreckage remains a mystery. He arrived at the pits, his uniform and linen helmet singed, his goggles missing a lens, but his great sense of humor remained intact. Carrying his steering wheel under one arm, he said, "This is all I could salvage from my racer."

Caracciola won at Monaco and Tunis, while Varzi was victorious at Tripoli.

That year's Eifelrennen was held in misting rain and fog. Caracciola led the early laps around the 14-mile Nürburgring until a broken shock absorber sidelined his Mercedes. Nuvolari took over the lead. But back down the foggy road, Rosemeyer was making an unbelievable charge. Rosemeyer caught Nuvolari and took the lead. As the fog thickened, Rosemeyer pulled away for a huge lead. The "Ring" was all but invisible, but Rosemeyer never slackened his pace. He took the checkered flag six minutes ahead of Nuvolari. His sensational victory gave rise to the title Nebelmeister – Master of the Mists.

Rosemeyer gets ready to make a practice run over the Roosevelt raceway course in preparation for the 1937 Vanderbilt Cup race. He was very popular with the American press and the fans. Rosemeyer led most of the contest to win the rich event. His Auto Union teammate, Ernst von Delius, is in the car behind Rosemeyer.

up their cars trying to catch his flying Auto Union. At the finish, he had a four-minute advantage over Stuck. This was a win for the ages, and it certainly established Rosemeyer and his tail-wagging Auto Union as the most formidable combination in Grand Prix racing.

With his two sensational back-to-back wins over the sinuous Ring, Rosemeyer was a step closer to realizing his dream. The great Caracciola could feel the championship slipping from his grasp.

Rosemeyer followed this home victory with another solid win at the Coppa Acerbo. On his lap of honor, fans said he saluted the place where he had crashed the previous year.

During the Swiss Grand Prix, held over the fast and treacherous Bremgarten course, Rosemeyer and Caracciola waged a fierce and bitter duel for the lead. Every time Rosemeyer thought he had Caracciola measured for the pass, the wily veteran jockeyed to block him. After 29 laps of this, Rosemeyer pressed Caracciola into making one of his rare mistakes. The Mercedes pilot bashed a wheel against a curb, giving the lead, the race and the European championship to his young nemesis. After only two years of competition, Rosemeyer was the Grand Prix ace of aces.

At the hotel that evening, Rosemeyer returned the swizzle stick to Caracciola. "Well done, dear fellow," Rosemeyer said, echoing Caracciola's words of advice. "But in future, don't just drive around the circuit. Use your head."

The European championship behind him, all that stood between Rosemeyer and the fulfillment of the second half of his dream – the German championship – was the Freiburg Hill Climb. He attacked the dangerously narrow, tree-lined, seven-mile Schauinsland course with his customary audacity. He hurtled into the sweeping, tricky Holzschlagermatten bend in a vicious powerslide. His racer exited the curve to thunderous cheers, the inside front tire slicing across the grass. He stopped the clocks at 7:59 flat for another new record. He had won the climb, the championship and his dream. Before the year was over, Rosemeyer won the Feldburg Hill Climb, and bested Nuvolari and his close friend and teammate Ernst von Delius in the

Even on the open highway, Rosemeyer never slowed for rain or fog. Once, while driving his Horch roadster along a foggy, unfamiliar country road with Elly by his side, he sped along at a breakneck pace. Elly admonished him to slow down. "Oh, calm down," he smiled. "I'm not going to hit that cyclist." Elly couldn't see a thing, but as they hustled on down the road another hundred yards, Rosemeyer eased the car to the center of the pavement, streaking by a bike rider that suddenly loomed up out of the murk. He would demonstrate this incredible ability numerous times.

ACE OF ACES

Rosemeyer should have won the Budapest Grand Prix. But a momentary mistake, coupled with a fired-up Nuvolari, put him 14 seconds behind the Italian at the finish.

When the circus returned to the Nürburgring for the German Grand Prix, Rosemeyer was in top form. He took the lead on lap 11, shattering the track record with a stunning 9:56.4 clocking. Other drivers blew

Italian GP at Monza.

Several months later, Rosemeyer and Caracciola patched up their differences. Some say it was at a dinner held by Nazi Propaganda Minster Josef Goebbels, while others say it was at Berlin's famous Roxy bar after the Goebbels party. In any case, Rosemeyer sought out Caracciola and the older man graciously accepted Rosemeyer's olive branch. A mutual respect grew out of their conversation. Caracciola came to value Rosemeyer's humor, even if he often became its target.

Apart from driving for the government-subsidized racing teams, neither Caracciola nor Rosemeyer had much truck with the Nazis. Caracciola refused to join the Nazi party. Rosemeyer seldom gave the fascist salute during the playing of "Deutschland uber Alles." When he did, it often turned into a wave directed at the crowd.

In 1937, Mercedes had a great advantage with their new 600-horsepower, supercharged, straight-eight W125. Rosemeyer waged an uphill battle from the start, but he certainly wasn't going to lie down.

He won the Eifelrennen – his third victory in a row at the Nürburgring – and repeated at the Coppa Acerbo. Rosemeyer could have won the Grosvernor Grand Prix in South Africa, too, but he allowed his young teammate, Ernst von Delius, to win. Delius was a reserve driver, and the victory allowed him to be considered for a regular position on the team.

At Avus, which now sported a newly built 43-degree banked north turn paved with bricks, Rosemeyer's streamlined Auto Union turned the fastest official lap of 171.74 mph. During practice, some stopwatches had him at over 176. Rosemeyer and Caracciola's streamlined cars had a tremendous battle in the first seven-lap heat, as they tore down the straights side-by-side at some 220 mph. Caracciola just managed to squeak past Rosemeyer at the finish. They averaged over 159 mph for the 82.12 miles. In the final, they went at it again, until Rosemeyer had to pit for repairs. Covered with oil, he fought his way back to finish fourth to Hermann Lang's Mercedes and his Auto Union teammates Delius and Rudi Hasse. Caracciola was a DNF.

The following paintings, which originally appeared in AQ Vol. 8 No. 1, are the work of Walter Gotschke. Above we see Caracciola leading Rosemeyer in the 1936 Swiss GP at Berne. Rosemeyer would burn through the 15th lap at a record-setting 105.42 mph and pull out a victory. The Auto Unions finished one-two-three.

In July, Rosemeyer and Delius journeyed to America for the Vanderbilt Cup race. Upon his arrival, Rosemeyer was chosen as the favorite to win. His first view of the Long Island course, with curves blinded by walls and fencing, gave him a start. Shaking his head, he referred to the track as "a double-cognac surprise."

In practice, Caracciola was the fastest, with Rosemeyer and Rex Mays next. But in the race, Rosemeyer drove with his usual abandon, sliding around the "curly course" in great drifts. He won by 50 seconds in front of Dick Seaman, with Mays third and Delius fourth. Caracciola had dropped out with supercharger trouble.

Then came the German Grand Prix. With three straight victories over the treacherous Ring, Rosemeyer was the prohibitive favorite. In practice he eclipsed his own record with a lap of 9:53.4. This was six seconds faster than the second-fastest driver Lang.

In the race, Rosemeyer raced superbly against Lang and Caracciola, until his slithering Auto Union and the road parted company. Regaining control, he proceeded to reel in the leaders until one of his tires blew out. A long pit stop dropped him from contention, but he never stopped trying, turning the fastest laps in the race. Caracciola won, with Brauchitsch second, only 15 seconds ahead of Rosemeyer.

Delius was badly injured in a crash with Seaman. Young Delius, the former reserve driver Rosemeyer had befriended, died during the night. Rosemeyer felt his loss immensely.

A LITTLE LUCK CAN'T HURT

Rosemeyer wasn't superstitious. His only talisman was the number 13. Elly often wore a scarf embroidered with his lucky number. However, after one particular hair-raising event, even the fearless warrior had to admit a flash of foreboding to Caracciola. "We cannot go on this way, Rudi. One of us will die. Then, after he is gone, the other will become champion of Europe once more."

For the third straight year, Rosemeyer won the Coppa Acerbo at Pescara. But thereafter, Caracciola and the Mercedes thunderbolt went on a rampage, winning the Swiss, Italian and Czechoslovakian events. With this burst of success, coupled with Rosemeyer suffering several mechanical failures, Caracciola wrapped up the European title.

The last race of the year was at the three-mile-plus, park-like course in Donington. Much has been said about that GP, the first of its kind in England. The racing press tried to prepare the British fans for what they were about to see. But nothing could compare with actually witnessing Rosemeyer and Brauchitsch battling side by side, nose to tail, jumping their monsters over Starkey Hill at 170 mph in a cloud of dust and burning rubber. During this frantic display, the two juggernauts were in one tire-smoking slide – first left, then right – all the way from Red Gate Bend to Coppice Corner, a distance of nearly half a lap. Both cars slid off the road several times, pitching dirt and grass into the frenzied crowd. The fans, initially watching in speechless awe, now stood cheering and shouting themselves hoarse. Finally, a blown tire ended Brauchitsch's chances, and Rosemeyer sped to a well-deserved victory. The usually sedate English crowd mobbed both men with congratulations.

A few days after returning to Germany, Rosemeyer launched his Auto Union streamliner down a blocked-off section of the Frankfurt-Darmstadt autobahn. When the run was over, he held every record from one kilometer to 10 miles in International Class B and C. His speed of 252.46 mph for the flying mile was the fastest yet recorded for a Grand Prix-chassied car. But during the flying five-kilometer run, fumes invaded the closed cockpit causing him to black out. Rosemeyer clung groggily to the steering wheel as the racer coasted nearly a mile before coming to a stop. He had to be lifted from the cockpit, but his new mark was 251.39 mph. Once again, Rosemeyer avoided seemingly certain disaster.

In November, Elly gave birth to a boy. There seemed no end to Rosemeyer's happiness. The proud parents asked the Nuvolaris to be their son's godparents.

SEEKING MORE SPEED

Rosemeyer told Tazio that Auto Union had a new car in the works that would raise the record for the flying mile to somewhere between 280 and 290 mph. Rosemeyer hinted that his goal was still higher. Because the world's land speed record was 311.42 mph, set by Captain George Eyston's massive eight-wheeled Thunderbolt utilizing two Rolls-Royce aero engines, Rosemeyer's news astounded Nuvolari. The runs would be held in late spring or during the summer.

But a few weeks later, Rosemeyer was informed that Mercedes intended to send Caracciola and a streamliner to the Frankfurt autobahn the last week in January 1938. Auto Union revised their schedule so that, if necessary, Rosemeyer could recapture his record on the same day.

Shortly after dawn on Jan. 28, 1938, bucking a tremendous wind, Caracciola rocketed down the autobahn setting a two-way average of 268.7 mph for the mile. The Mercedes had retaken the record. Rosemeyer couldn't believe the news. How had he driven so fast

Rosemeyer is depicted here in the aerodynamic A.V.U.S. C-Type that he used to break 17 records at the German Record Week on the Frankfurt-Darmstadt autobahn.

During the first heat of the 1937 Avusrennen, Caracciola in car no. 35 and Rosemeyer in no. 31 fly around the North Curve. Their streamlined cars reached 220 mph on the straights. Caracciola barely nipped Rosemeyer (above) to win this heat.

on such a terrible day?

By midmorning Rosemeyer was warming up the Auto Union streamliner for his own attempt. The wind had become gusty – even worse than it had been for Caracciola. On the outward practice run Rosemeyer clocked 244. He returned to the starting line at a stunning 269.

Caracciola and Brauchitsch were waiting for him. "Herr Record Breaker!" Rosemeyer exclaimed with a grin as Caracciola walked over to the car. Someone mentioned that the wind was rising. "There is only one bad place," Rosemeyer responded, "at the Morfelden clearing just before the long underpass. I'll be all right. I'm one of the lucky ones."

Years later, Caracciola explained to his American friend Ted Everroade about that morning. "I wanted to

say something to Bernd about the danger, [that] maybe he should postpone the run," Caracciola said. "But someone walked up to tell him something just then and I walked away. What could I have said to another brave driver? He knew what we were facing."

Rosemeyer climbed into his streamliner, left the control point, and was soon up to speed. The road constricted into a narrow band of concrete.

Dr. Feuereissen listened intently on the phone as observers reported the thundering Auto Union's progress from various checkpoints. From the short intervals between the reports and the shrill exhaust note coming from the car as Rosemeyer shot past each observer, Feuereissen knew the car was traveling over 280 mph. At kilometer post 9.2, the observer suddenly screamed into his phone, "The car is crashing!"

Feuereissen and Rosemeyer's mechanic Ludwig Sebastian rushed to the scene. They hoped against their rising fears that Rosemeyer would be standing there, steering wheel in hand, a boyish grin on his face. But all hope was gone when they reached the Morfelden clearing. The landscape resembled the site of a plane crash, aluminum debris scattered everywhere. The chassis was found 600 yards farther down the road.

Rosemeyer was found high above the autobahn, lying on his back under the trees. There was not a mark on him. His bright eyes stared at Feuereissen and Sebastian. For an instant, he seemed to be smiling at his friends, but their hearts were only seeing what they hoped for most. The idol of German youth, the boy wonder of Grand Prix racing, was dead at 28. His prophesy to Caracciola had come to pass.

Rosemeyer readies for his try at breaking Caracciola's just-established speed record in the 545hp R-Type. The car was designed for reducing wind resistance, but it high-speed stability was jeopardized. A cross-wind would cause a fatal crash.

Over the 70 years since that fateful morning, countless theories have been brought forth as to what caused the accident. In the end, the most likely explanation was simply a gale-force wind that was reported at that very moment at the local airport.

How good was Rosemeyer? His record lap of 105.6 mph at the 1936 Swiss Grand Prix was never broken. And the Bremgarten course remained in use through 1954. His 171.74-mph lap of Avus stood as the fastest closed course speed in all forms of racing for 20 years.

To the racing world, not unlike the death of America's Frank Lockhart, Rosemeyer's loss seemed to be such a waste of a truly gifted driver. He remains the fearless, happy warrior who inspired awe and admiration in even his most bitter rivals.

SS Sports Cars
The SS90 and SS100

T he rise of Jaguar Cars from humble beginnings in the 1920s has a Cinderella-like aura to it in the way in which it grew at a time when so many rivals in England fell by the wayside. And like all good stories, it had the most unlikely of beginnings. At first only two people were involved: two men named William, as it happened – William Lyons and William Walmsley, who was 10 years Lyons' senior.

BY GAVIN FARMER

They were living and working in the Lancashire city of Blackpool, Britain's favorite holiday destination with its long promenade of amusement arcades on the sea front. Quite by chance, Lyons saw what was a delightfully stylish sidecar attached to a war surplus Triumph motorcycle and, intrigued, walked into the shed where the sidecars were being made. There he met Walmsley. The two men developed a rapport and Lyons instinctively knew that here was his destiny.

On Lyons' 21st birthday, Sept. 4, 1922, he and Walmsley officially formed a partnership and the Swallow Sidecar Company was born. Business grew rapidly and soon the premises at Bloomfield Road, Blackpool, were woefully inadequate, and even though the partners leased two more buildings, it was clear that a large, single, consolidated site was urgently required. This was found in Cocker Street and in mid-1926 the move was made.

With the motorcycle sidecar business booming, Lyons turned his attention to motor cars and in par-

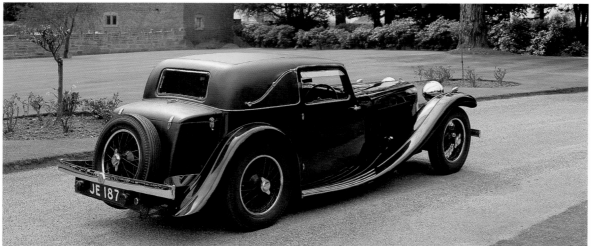

The SS1 coupe set the style even if it did not have quite the performance its appearance suggested. Shown here: The 1932-33 SS1 fixed-head coupe.

ticular the Austin 7, because he had recently bought a second-hand example and believed its styling could be improved. One day, he noticed that new employee Cyril Holland had drawn a rough sketch of a two-seater that he asked to have redrawn properly "to suit the dimensions of an Austin 7 chassis." The next problem was acquiring a chassis, but business colleague Sydney Parker was persuaded to locate one for Lyons that was delivered to the Cocker Street premises in January 1927. Six months later the first Austin-Swallow was announced.

As was common with coachbuilders at the time, it had an aluminium body formed over an ash frame. Mechanically it was pure Austin 7 because Swallow did not have the resources to carry out such work, but the style of the body was a revelation by comparison with the ultra-utilitarian "style" of the Longbridge product.

Arrangements were made within the Cocker Street premises to produce the bodies in quantity, but the paint shop became the bottleneck as it could only cater for two cars per day. This was clearly not enough as Swallow dealers in Manchester and Bolton (Sydney Parker) and Blackpool (Brown and Mallalieu) wanted more stock. With P.J. Evans in Birmingham and Henleys in London – they placed an order for 500 cars at the rate of 20 per week – coming on board, some-

thing needed to be done, and quickly.

Lyons, always with an eye on the future, decided that they would have to move from Blackpool to the Midlands where the British car industry was centered if they were ever going to continue to grow. After some searching, a site was found at Foleshill, Coventry, that had been a shell-filling factory during World War I. The price was right for Lyons and a lease was signed immediately. The 140-mile move was made during November 1928 with many loyal employees going along, including Cyril Holland, Harry Gill, George Lee, Charlie Atkinson, Norman Holt, the Thacker and Marsh brothers, Jack Beardsley and many others.

Joining the Austin-Swallow that was being made at the rate of up to 50 units a week were the Fiat 509A, the Standard 9 and Swift 10 announced in 1929, the Wolseley Hornet in 1930, the Standard 16 in 1931, and the Wolseley Hornet Special in 1932. All were distinctly ordinary cars that, in their original form, lacked any real sense of style. Only the Standards were to be made in any numbers after the Austin.

What was considered the first "Jaguar" engine, the 2 1/2 -liter overhead-valve engine powered SS Jaguar saloons and tourers beginning with 1936 models. The 2663cc engine also powered the accomplished SS Jaguar 100 two-seater sports in 1936. A 3485cc version was found in SS 100s beginning in 1938. Shown above: The 1936 SS Jaguar 2 1/2-liter tourer.

Lyons fell out with Sir Herbert Austin but formed a symbiotic relationship with the autocratic John Black at the Standard Motor Company. It was here that Lyons was able to source rolling chassis developed for the Standard 16hp and made to his specifications – downswept in the center, the engine was mounted well back and the springs were outside the frame members – as well as engines, gearboxes and running gear. As Paul Skilleter wrote in *Jaguar Sports Cars*, "Although the Swallow Hornets had six-cylinder (sohc) engines in their spidery Wolseley chassis, it was undoubtedly the Standard Swallow 16hp that pointed the way ahead most surely. It, too, had a six-cylinder engine, and it was this tough, seven-bearing 2054cc unit that was to play an important part in Swallow's transition from

Shown here: Close-up views of the sporty 1937 SS Jaguar 100. When the SS 100 model range was announced in September 1935, the 100 designation was given not only because it had 100 bhp under the bonnet (in fact, 104 bhp was produced), but because it was a genuine 100 mph car.

coachbuilder to car manufacturer."

Cyril Holland, meanwhile, penned a low, rakish two-door two-seater that was announced in October 1931 and was badged "SS" with a deliberate full stop after each S. The two major weekly motoring magazines in England, *The Autocar* and *The Motor*, gave the new SS 1 tremendous coverage, *The Autocar*'s article including a fine cutaway drawing by its technical artist Max Millar.

With the approval of Edward (Ted) Grinham, chief engineer at Standard, all the SS engines had an aluminium alloy cylinder head cast by the Coventry Motor Cylinder Company. It was through this company Lyons met and was impressed by independent engine consultant Harry Weslake.

On Oct. 26, 1933, Lyons registered the subsidiary company SS Cars Limited.

Debate has ensued since as to whether SS stood for Standard-Swallow or Special Standard. Remembering his meeting with Weslake two years previously, Lyons contacted him and requested he design and develop a completely new overhead-valve cylinder head to fit the Standard six-cylinder engine block. All this frantic activity led Lyons to create an "engineering" department at SS Cars Ltd., which meant that he would require a qualified engineer. His contacts at Standard Motors, Ted Grinham and Les Dawtrey, suggested a precocious young fellow who had impressed them when working at Humber, William Heynes; he arrived at SS Cars Ltd. in April 1935. In January 1935, Walmsley resigned and so Lyons, now in total control, turned SS Cars Ltd. into a public company and Swallow Coachbuilding Co. (1935) was formed to continue the sidecar business.

In March 1935 the SS 90 sports car had been announced along with the SS 1 drophead coupe. The SS 90 was built on a shortened SS 1 chassis having some 15-inches removed from the center section, leaving a

wheelbase of 104 inches with the front and rear wheel tracks at 54 inches. With twin RAG carburettors and a 7.0:1 compression, the 2663cc six-cylinder side-valve engine (SS Cars always referred to it as a 2 1/2 liter) and its 73 x 106mm cylinder dimensions proved to be a willing powerhouse. Intriguingly, no power output figures were ever released officially but reliable "guesstimates" put its power at 75 bhp at 4500 rpm. Its chassis retained the semi-elliptic leaf spring front and rear suspension but added adjustable (from the cockpit) Andre Telecontrol dampers. In addition it used the SS 1 Bendix duo-servo cable operated brakes with their 12-inch diameter drums, as well as Rudge-Whitworth knock-off wire spoke wheels shod with 5.25 x 18 Dunlop tires. The four-speed gearbox was fitted with a specially made remote floor shift lever. Using the higher of the two rear axle ratios available, 3.75 instead of 4.25:1, *The Autocar* surmised in its report (not actually a full road test) that the SS 90 would achieve 90 mph as its name implied.

What set it apart from practically every other sports car available at the time was its combination of svelte styling – a collaboration between Holland and Lyons – with excellent performance, good handling and an astonishingly low price, just £395 (approx. $1,990). By way of comparison, the contemporary Frazer Nash BMW 319 that offered similar performance carried a retail price from AFN Ltd. of £460 (approx. $2,318).

Only 22 SS 90s were built before it was superceded by the virtually identical SS 100 that was announced in September 1935 as a 1936 model. With this announcement came a new name – Jaguar – and the full stops between the letters were dropped, so by the time it was in actual production it was known as the SS 100 Jaguar.

Newcomer Heynes had done a remarkable job of preparing the 1936 models in less than six months from his arrival. This task involved the redesign of certain components of the chassis, suspension, steering and brakes to suit, as well as liaise with Weslake who was developing the overhead-valve conversion that also was ready to come on-stream for the 1936 season.

The conversion of the engine was very professional in its execution and one that filled both Lyons and

Previous page, above and opposite: The magnificent SS 100 of 1938. The elegant coupe is reminiscent of the Bugatti Atalante.

Weslake with pride. Weslake retained the bottom end of the Standard engine because its rigid cast iron block and seven-bearing crankshaft were more than adequate for the task, although the pistons and connecting rods were redesigned and used different materials. He even retained the chain-driven side-mounted camshaft. Long pushrods were used to operate single (large) intake and exhaust valves per cylinder that were located on a rocker shaft bolted to pedestals in the head casting; a simple screw-and-nut adjusted the tappets. The ports were reshaped as were the combustion chambers, the compression was set at 6.4:1 and twin 1 1/4-inch SU carburettors supplied the intake mixture in place of the unreliable RAG units used previously. The porting was a little unusual insofar as there was an internal gallery cast into the head and the carburettors that were bolted directly to the nearside head face fed the gallery, which meant that there was no actual intake manifold. The inlet ports were short while the exhaust ports that led

to the off-side of the engine were much longer.

Checked by Heynes on the company's new engine test stand, Weslake's 2.7-liter six developed 105 bhp at 4500 rpm.

Although the SS 100 looked like the SS 90, there were in fact many detail changes, all generally for the better. A Burman Douglas worm-and-nut steering box was now specified along with Girling rod-operated brakes in place of the Bendix cable system; trunnion bearings replaced shackles on the rear of the front semi-elliptic springs together with a combination of Luvax hydraulic and Hartford friction dampers on the front axle. The actual chassis frame of the SS 100 dated back to the SS 1.

The Motor carried out a full road test in its May 25, 1937, issue, more than 18 months after the roadster had been announced. The test recorded some very fast times for a production sports car circa 1937. Its maximum speed was timed at 96 mph with 73 mph

and 46 mph available at the 4500 rpm redline in third and second gears respectively. Acceleration from 0-50 mph took 8.25 seconds, to 60 mph 12.8 seconds, and the standing start quarter mile was dispatched in 18.6 seconds. SS Cars had said the up-rated sports roadster was "primarily intended for competition work."

Journalists noted of the SS 100 that "the car was not classed as a racer by its makers, but many of the qualities of the thoroughbred automobile are to be found in its make up." They further added, "In keeping with such performance is the fact that steering is rock steady, the springing is reasonably comfortable and the brakes are not only powerful, but they never cause the driver any qualms." In conclusion: "Altogether an exceedingly attractive sports car which, considering the performance and general specification, is modestly priced at £395."

In September 1937 the range of SS Jaguars – 1 1/2 and 2 1/2 four-and six-cylinder models – segued into 1938 with a new engine added to the range, a 3 1/2-liter unit that Heynes had developed from the Standard and Weslake ideas embodied in the 2 1/2-liter unit. With a bore and stroke of 82 x 110 mm, it displaced a swept volume of 3485 cc and developed 125 bhp at 4500 rpm. Externally the major difference between the two six-cylinder engines was the twin triple-branch exhaust manifolds on the bigger unit, but this manifold was soon adopted by the smaller engine as the two engines were produced alongside each other.

Again *The Motor* and *The Autocar* were enthusiastic in their appraisal of the SS 100 Jaguar roadster, both recording a maximum speed that was timed at 101.12 mph. *The Motor* published figures of 7.1 and 10.4 seconds for the 0-50 mph and 0-60 mph sprints respectively; 30-50 mph passing acceleration took 7.3 sec-

onds in top (4th) gear and 5.9 seconds in third; and the standing quarter mile was covered in 17.1 seconds.

The Motor said of the SS 100 3 1/2-liter sports car in its July 12, 1938, issue: "To drive the 100 is to enjoy an experience unlikely to be forgotten for many a day to come. It is not merely that the car provides an exceptional performance through the gears, that the roadholding is up to the speed of the car and that the brakes are among the best ever tested, but the fact that a complete absence of temperament and very great flexibility are among its assets."

What was astonishing was that SS Cars Ltd. set a recommended retail price of £445 (approx. $2,242).

In late 1938, Walter Hassan joined SS Cars to work as the company's chief experimental engineer liaising with Bill Heynes in the engineering department such as it was (consisting of little more than an engine test bed, some welding equipment, tools and a hoist). Hassan and Heynes had met when the former was preparing Edgar Wadsworth's SS 100 for competition and developed a mutual respect for each other. These two talented engineers would form the nucleus of the engineering future for the young company.

Between late 1935 and the end of 1939, the company built only 308 SS 100 roadsters, 191 with the 2 1/2-liter engine, and 117 with the 3 1/2-liter unit. Today, any SS 90 and SS 100 is a much sought-after collector car.

The company mothballed its car body-making equipment when war erupted in Europe, switching over to war work, making hundreds of sidecars and trailers by the thousands for the Allies, plus repair work on damaged Whitley bombers. With peace in sight, Lyons made a decision that was critical to the future of his company – he changed its name. Between 1933 and 1945 the initials SS had become known for rather sinister and unsavory activities against humanity, so a company name change was inevitable. In February 1945, Lyons applied to use the marque name Jaguar as the new company name, and in March the name Jaguar Cars Limited was registered with plans for a completely new engine, new chassis and new body designs for the world to enjoy and appreciate.

The 1939 SS 100 shown here was the final SS Jaguar sports model to be produced. Ten years would elapse before the market saw another sports car from the company.

William Lyons was no engineering or inventive genius. His ability lay in seeing an opportunity and pursuing it with all his energy and dedication, and at the same time cannily choosing talented people who were similarly dedicated to helping him realize his dreams.

THE SS 90 AND SS 100 JAGUARS IN COMPETITION

With such alluring style and an excellent power-to-weight ratio, especially in the 3 1/2-liter SS 100, nobody was surprised when examples began appearing in competitive events around England. The first notable success came with Tommy and Elsie Wisdom driving a factory-owned 2 1/2-liter SS 100 competing in the 1936 International Alpine Trial, where they won the Glacier Cup. They also claimed a moral victory over the winning Bugatti because they lost no points whatsoever on the road section. This win by a car from the tiny Coventry company soon made people sit up and take notice of its

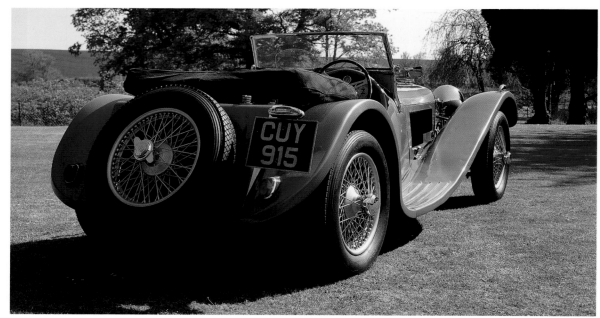

achievements. Wisdom was an ideal driver for Lyons. He was a journalist for the *Daily Herald* and *Sporting Life* and was an experienced race and rally driver who knew how to get the best out of a car.

The car that the Wisdoms drove was known irreverently at the works as "Old Number 8" because it was built on chassis number 18008 and was the development hack on which new ideas were tried. It bore the registration number BWK77 and has survived to this day.

Through 1936, BWK77 was driven by S. H. "Sammy" Newsome and Tommy Wisdom with Newsome generally driving it in hillclimbs and Wisdom in rallies and track events. Other SS 100s appeared in rallies and hillclimbs all over England as well as at the Marne Grand Prix for sports cars at Rheims, where it was driven by an Australian, F.J. McEvoy, and won the 2- to 3-liter class. SS 100s were also successful at the famous Brooklands circuit in Surrey and in the MCC High Speed Trial.

Even greater success was enjoyed by SS 100s the following year with works entries in the RAC Rally held in May – drivers Wisdom, Rankin, Jacobs and Lewis – but they were beaten by Jack Harrop in his privately entered SS 100 roadster. The SS Cars team, however, won the Manufacturer's Team Prize.

The Welsh Rally was another major benefit for the young company, with Jacobs' SS 100 putting up the best overall performance. Jacobs, Rankin and Matthews again took the Manufacturer's Team Prize for SS Cars.

Old Number 8 was heavily modified for the meeting at Brooklands, sporting an experimental cylinder head with a 10.5:1 compression ratio that required a methanol-based fuel; power output was reportedly 150 bhp. It managed to lap the rough outer circuit at 118 mph. In the Long Handicap it won by an amazing 12 seconds from the next car.

Probably the highlight of the year for SS Cars was the victory by Casimiro de Oliveira in the Vila Real race, where he came from behind to defeat an Adler, BMW and Alfa Romeo by one second after 90 miles of racing. It was most likely SS Cars' first outright win in racing on the Continent.

If 1937 was good, then 1938 was even better. Jack Harrop brought his SS 100 home first in class in the RAC Rally, while two months later Mrs. Hetherington came second in her class in the Welsh Rally, winning the Lady's Award. At the SS Car Club meeting at Donington, William Lyons won his race against Heynes and Newsome. The car club was very active with social and competitive events held regularly and undoubtedly helped greatly in spreading the word about the company's products. Newsome in BWK77 competed at the Shelsley Walsh hillclimb but his times were uncompetitive due to a problem with the gearbox.

One enthusiastic SS 100 owner was Paul Marx who took his car to America in 1937 where he met the Collier brothers and others associated with the Automobile Racing Club of America (ARCA) and finished 7th in their 1938 "championship."

The Paris-Nice trial attracted SS 100 entries from Wisdom, Vernon and Pycroft, with Wisdom actually running a 2 1/2-liter version. No podium finishes were obtained, but in some of the individual events of the trial the drivers proved to be competitive.

The 1939 RAC Rally, the last to be held for several years, saw Newsome gain second place in the Open Cars section with a bevy of other SS 100s competing in the event. In June, Old Number 8 had its last outing at Shelsley Walsh and was substantially modified for the event by running special domed pistons that raised its compression ratio to 14:1 and required a methanol-blend fuel to produce 169 bhp at 4250 rpm. Newsome won the unsupercharged class quite easily at the climb. Wisdom later drove it at Brooklands using a 3:1 rear axle ratio and in practice recorded a lap of 125 mph; unfortunately, the crankshaft broke during the race.

After the war, Old Number 8 resumed racing in a limited way, bearing in mind the deprivations of the times. The car was eventually discarded only to re-appear many years later in Liverpool – nobody knows how it got there – to be lovingly restored by David Barker.

THE JAGUAR NAME

Lyons was keen to give his cars actual names instead of letters and numbers as had been the case for the first four years of his company's existence. He wanted a name that would suggest power and sleekness so he asked various staff members to come up with some animal, bird and place names that could be suitable. One name kept being mentioned – Jaguar – which grabbed Lyons' attention, and then he remembered stories by childhood friend Arnold Breakell who had worked as a mechanic on Armstrong-Siddeley aero engines during World War 1, one of which was called "Jaguar." That settled it. Lyons would adopt the name and image of the Jaguar, one of the fastest and sleekest animals on earth.

THE SCARISBRICK–COLE SS 100 ROADSTER

BY JOHN NORCIA AND TRACY POWELL

Like the 2 1/2-liter cars of 1935-38, the 3 1/2-liter quickly became the favorite of British sportsman drivers. In all, 117 were produced from 1938-39, with this car, chassis number 39086, built in October 1938. Chassis no. 39086 was dispatched to Henley's on Oct. 11, 1938, and later delivered to Sir Everard Talbot Scarisbrick, lord of Scarisbrick Manor, and registered by Devon County Council as FXX 539. It is unknown if Sir Everard ever entered the car in competition.

During the war years, the car was put in storage, where it remained until 1949. In that year, 39086 was purchased by Tommy Cole, an up-and-coming British racecar driver, and shipped to New York to compete in the first Bridgehampton road race. (Bridgehampton was the second major road race held in the United States after World War II, and a revival of the road-racing sport on Long Island after a lapse of 29 years.) The list of driver entries included George Rand and George Huntoon, both successful in '30s road races, and Sam Collier and Briggs Cunningham, with future "names" John Fitch, Tommy Cole and Paul O'Shea appearing for the first time.

Tommy Cole's SS 100 entry was confirmed by promoter and Bridgehampton historian Jim Shelly. Also, in his excellent history of Bridgehampton racing, Joel Finn writes that the car had arrived only two days before the race on the *Queen Mary* and was totally unprepared for racing as a result of years in storage. It spent Friday night in Jim McGee's garage in Watermill and was driven to 2nd place in the 100-mile race by Cole. Near the end of the race, Cole was running 2nd and gaining on the leader Huntoon in his supercharged Alfa Romeo, but an encounter with the hay bales delayed him long enough for Huntoon to finish first. The checkered flag was given to Huntoon, Cole and Sam Collier, in that order.

After the excitement at Bridgehampton, 39086 was raced in many other events of that era. Finally, in the late 1950s, the stripped-down, raced-out and neglected car came under the ownership of Ed Bond of Saybrook, Conn., who purchased the "remains" in Alabama. It is not known how the car got to Alabama.

That next owner, Russ Sceli of Canton, Conn., purchased 39086 in 1960 and promptly initiated restoration. Sceli was a notable figure in the formation of the SCCA and had raced a Bugatti T57 in the first Seneca Cup Race at Watkins Glen in 1949. Sceli was a dealer in Bugattis and according to author Karl Ludvigsen in *Hemmings*, "Russ Sceli was a major carrier of the

sports car bacillus infecting many Americans in the early '50s."

Sceli states in his registration document dated April 1, 1964, submitted to the SS 100 registrar for the Classic Jaguar Association, that he completely rebuilt 39086 in 1961-62. The original instruments were beyond repair and replaced with new XK120 Smiths gauges, speedometer and tachometer in a new engine-turned panel. A Scintilla magneto replaced the distributor and coil. Sceli states that he purchased the last set of new wings from the factory and completely rebuilt the engine, gearbox and differential. With the car now in "mint" condition, Sceli entered the car in the 1963 Westport (Conn.) Concours, winning Best of Show.

A notation on Sceli's registration document, presumably made by the registrar, states that the car was listed for sale by a New York City car dealer in 1966. From New York City the car made its way to Cleveland, owned by Carlton Coolege. In 1975, Coolege and 39086 moved to San Francisco.

In late 1975 the car was purchased from Coolege by John A. Norcia, Canton, Ohio, the present owner. On its trip from California back to Ohio, it was unloaded briefly at the Barrett-Jackson Auction, where someone took a photograph, which appeared in the *CJA Newsletter* with a request for identification.

The car was received in running condition but was

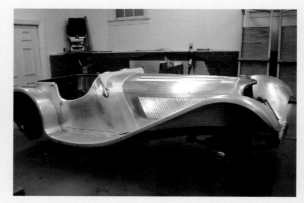

This 3 1/2-liter SS 100, originally built in October 1938, found its way to enthusiast John Norcia. Norcia oversaw the meticulous restoration, in progress above and completed (opposite).

otherwise a collection of noticeably incorrect components and restoration decisions. It remained in storage until 1990 when a serious search for correct spares and restoration began. Fortunately, all the major components, so to speak, were there, but it took 15 years to collect all the correct bits required for the restoration.

"The biggest challenge is keeping the commitment to do whatever is necessary as many times as necessary to bring the restoration to the highest level. When you are halfway through the project and it looks overwhelming, the romance goes away and you really have to stay committed to see that every detail is correct."

— *John Norcia*

Although much of the wooden subframe and some of the body panels needed repair, Sceli's wings were in reasonably good condition with only minor repair required. The bodywork was completely hand-straightened and metal-finished to perfection. This time-consuming procedure was necessary, as the paint color decision was black, perhaps the most unforgiving color as it relates to revealing flaws.

While the bodywork was sent off to the paint shop in pieces, the focus was now on the drivetrain, which, with the exception of a growling first gear, was in excellent condition. Likewise, the engine, which upon

disassembly for inspection showed no signs of wear, was carefully reassembled with new seals and gaskets. An oiling modification that provides increased lubrication to the top end, probably made by Tommy Cole, was left in place.

With the car assembled except for wings, running and road testing was completed, and trim work followed. The restoration of 39086 was completed in late 2007.

"If you are the restorer, you are doing it primarily for your own satisfaction," Norcia said. "You are giving a new and better life to this piece of rolling art." △○

"In the 3 1/2-litre 100 model open two seater, SS Cars Ltd. have certainly produced a machine to covet."

— The Autocar, Sept. 9, 1938

Art Gallery with
Steve Anderson
A Designer's Documentary

When he's not busy at his full-time job in GM's Advanced Design studios in Los Angeles, restoring an old house or tinkering with his '61 E-type Jaguar, Steve Anderson is creating what he calls "artistic documentary."

BY TRACY POWELL

If technical accuracy is your bent when it comes to memorializing your car, then Steve Anderson is your man. Whether captured in profile (by far the most popular) or multiple views, Anderson's documentary illustrations are in demand.

"The types of commission I get varies," Anderson said. "I enjoy working with the guy who has one car, and every four or five years he gives me a call and wants me to do his new car. At the moment I'm working with a collector in Mexico who is having me do upwards of 20 illustrations for a permanent place in his collection."

Anderson uses the same basic automotive design technique that he started with in the early '90s. The technique utilizes a combination of tools including Prismacolor pencils, airbrush, gouache paint, and marker. For the majority of his work, the process begins by hand, creating a line drawing, rendering it out and airbrushing it, creating several different plates. Each plate is a different element of the car: the body color as one plate, the wheels one plate, the interior another plate and so on. He then scans these into Adobe Photoshop and builds it out, performing color corrections, highlight balancing, and any proportional adjustments that need made. This is then printed using a giclee printer. The final 10 percent is done by hand, when he applies gouache and uses colored pencils to pop out the line work.

"Regarding the use of Photoshop, I'm constantly gelling between how much emphasis to place on one end and the other," Anderson said. "Some pieces may be more digitally intensive than others, but ultimately I strive to maintain that hand-created effect. That's why you'll still see things like a little airbrush texture in the work.

"I don't like digital artwork that much because it seems a bit sterile and removed. I try to only use digital as a means of bringing it all together. A lot of that comes from experiencing fatigue, the drop of a brush at 2 a.m. when you're almost to the end, and you ruin eight or nine hours worth of work. So using Photoshop is a good safety net at best."

Anderson's unique approach has been featured in

a handful of magazines, including *The Robb Report Collection*. His work as staff illustrator for *Excellence* and *Forza Magazine* has met with approval and granted license for print by Dr. Ing. H.c.F. Porsche AG and Ferrari S.p.A. respectively.

"I don't consider what I do fine art," noted Anderson. "It's best described as highly accurate technical illustration. I'll often recommend fellow artists when the client's desires are for a more expressive, 'setting oriented' approach. For me, the true beauty is the car: its surfaces, details and care that went into its creation."

A DESIGNER'S LIFE

Anderson's earliest automotive influence came from his grandfather. His early years were spent growing up in Pasadena, Calif., where his grandfather "dragged me to every sanctioned motor sport event that you could find. In the early '70s, the Long Beach Grand Prix, the Riverside races, Can Am, Trans Am, stock cars. Ontario was alive and kicking back then and they hosted NHRA and maybe Winston Cup. I was exposed to a wide variety of motor

'78 Ferrari 308 GTS

do. From that point on, everything I did was aimed at getting to the point where this passion of mine – mixing my love of cars and art and design – developed into a career."

In high school his family relocated to Spokane, Wash., which meant he no longer had the ability to tie into Art Center. But he took as much art as possible in the public school curriculum and even helped design his drafting courses in industrial arts. That helped gear him up for the automotive industry. His teacher and the career counselor at the high school endorsed what he did and let him run with it. For Anderson, the affirmation of his abilities, as well as the results that followed, proved a great stimulus.

After high school Anderson attended a small private college in Washington.

"At that point I realized that car design is a small field and that I may not get through," Anderson said. "But there's also the bigger question of needing to better understand for whom you are designing and what you are creating that effects the marketplace. I wasn't going to design in a vacuum and create Steve Anderson cars all day long."

Anderson received a four-year degree in business management with a concentration on marketing and communications. His tenure at that school provided Anderson with the academic requirements that prepared him to attend Art Center. What's more, with his management degree, Anderson had created, in himself, a more marketable product. Noted Anderson: "The reality is, automakers are looking for well-rounded individuals that know and appreciate all aspects of the business."

His first job out of Art Center was with the Volkswagen design studios in Los Angeles.

"I was fortunate in that I joined a team that was led by J. Mays and Freeman Thomas," Anderson said. "Freeman was the designer of the TT and is now the director of concept development at Ford on the West Coast. Freeman is as avid a Porsche enthusiast as you'll ever find. That's really where I cut my teeth in terms of the Porsche community and starting to develop this documentary style of art."

After reading *Excellence Was Expected* by Karl

sports. That's what whetted my appetite for a life of cars, and I pretty much had a fascination with anything that had four wheels."

His family lived on the same street of a dealership owner. One of his favorite hobbies involved waiting at the end of each day for the dealer to come home, watching to see what new car he was driving. Anderson says that he was the only kid sitting on the curb trying to figure out if it was a normally aspirated Porsche or a turbo coming up the road.

Also, and perhaps most important, Anderson was exposed at an early age to Art Center College of Design. His artistic bent was noticed in grade school, and, at age 10, he was invited to a specialized art program organized by the Pasadena school district during the summer. Part of the program included a tour of Art Center, which began in the Transportation Department. That first stop was all it took for Anderson – he had seen enough.

"I asked my teacher if they could just come get me when they were through with the tour," Anderson said. "That was where I wanted to spend my hour. At that moment I decided that my passion for art and cars would be one and the same; I knew what I wanted to

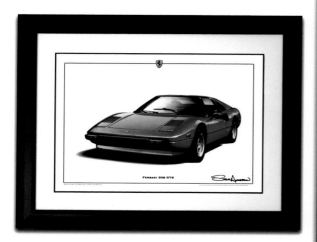

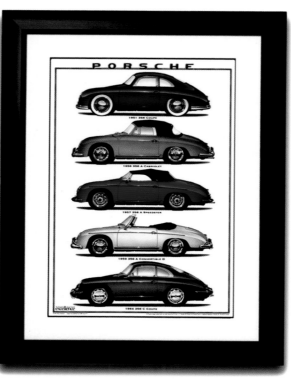

Anderson was trying to accomplish and how to best achieve that end. His new pastime took off from there.

"At the Porsche Club of America meets in the Santa Barbara region, people started hearing about what I was doing," Anderson said. "Word of mouth started growing and I began taking orders to create this artistic documentation for car owners."

Anderson has tried to stay focused on Porsche, Ferrari and Corvette. In the course of doing these pieces, he notes, the artist must intimately know the subject, "because what I'm trying to do is not fantasy portrayal. Instead I am trying to factually portray the car. People seemingly like having the two opposites: the John Marsh style, with the car at riverside in a picnic setting, or something to that effect; and the strict documentary approach of their vehicle that charts their ownership."

At the present, about 65 percent of the Anderson's commissions are from return customers, many of whom have ordered eight to 10 pieces over the years.

PERSONAL NOTES

Anderson, 41, lives in San Marino, Calif., with his wife and their five children ranging in ages from 3 to 14. One would think that holding down a full-time job (he has worked in GM's Advanced Design studios for almost eight years) and

Ludvigsen (originally published by Automobile Quarterly) and seeing Ken Rush's illustrations in that book, Anderson first thought of doing something along those lines. He decided to give it a try, drawing his first Porsche. Thomas assisted in formulizing what

keeping up with his large household doesn't leave time for much else. Then you realize that Anderson simply finds the time.

"I'll spend maybe 10 hours this weekend doing work on my illustrations," he said. "About four evenings during any given week I'll sit down around 9 p.m., after the kids are in bed and my wife is wiped

ties for the do-it-yourselfer in Anderson, allowing him to experiment in projects such as finish carpentry.

"I like learning about carpentry and the tricks that are used," Anderson said. "That's an escape for me, away from the car thing, and it's a way to exercise some of that unused architectural interest in me. Aside from that I have a '61 E-type roadster that I dink

around with when time permits."

Skateboarding is another interest. Whether during weekday lunch hours or on the weekends with his kids, Anderson notes that skateboarding is the only exercise he gets. Of course, that would refer to physical exercise; mental – or creative – exercise he gets in abundance. ◢◣

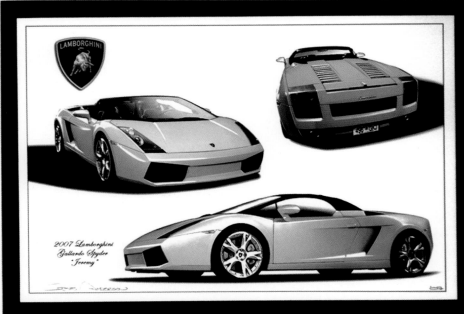

2007 Lamborghini
Gallardo Spyder
"Jeremy"

1971 FIAT 500L
s/n: 6097026
Exterior: Rosso
Interior: Camel
Owner: Ali Kasikci

out and she goes to bed, and I'll stay up until midnight or one o'clock working. It's nice quiet time. My boss probably wouldn't want to hear it, but I'm doing what I really want to do, not what I'm being asked to do. It's really enjoyable to unwind."

At the top of his list of influences are his mother, whose support at an early age helped set Anderson's life course, his aforementioned grandfather, and two favorite Art Center instructors: Richard Pietruska and Craig Mullen.

In addition to his design and art endeavors, Anderson has an interest in home renovation and restoration. Living in an older home presents countless opportuni-

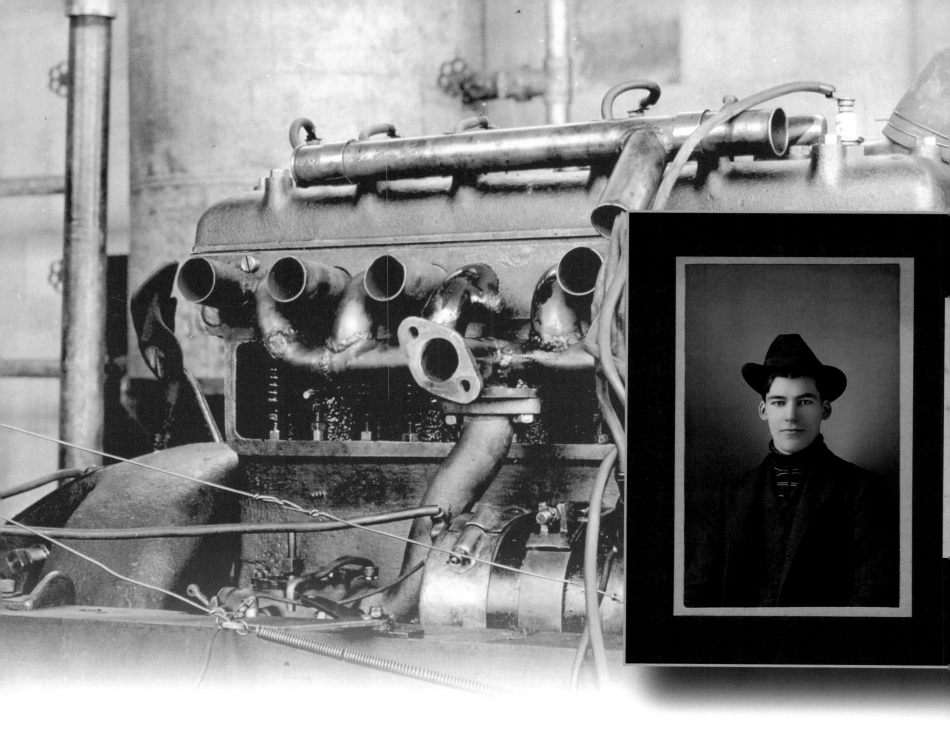

E.J. Hall's
Life of Power

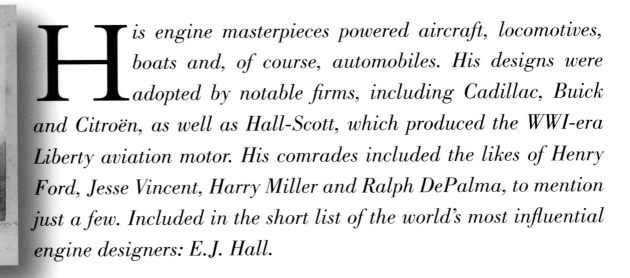

His engine masterpieces powered aircraft, locomotives, boats and, of course, automobiles. His designs were adopted by notable firms, including Cadillac, Buick and Citroën, as well as Hall-Scott, which produced the WWI-era Liberty aviation motor. His comrades included the likes of Henry Ford, Jesse Vincent, Harry Miller and Ralph DePalma, to mention just a few. Included in the short list of the world's most influential engine designers: E.J. Hall.

BY RIC A. DIAS

Elbert John Hall was born on April 8, 1882, in San Jose, Calif., to farmer parents. As true with many rural children of the period, Elbert ended his formal education early, after the 7th grade. Concerning his classroom performance, the *San Jose Mercury Herald* reported that the young Hall "listened intently to his teacher, when it was urgently necessary, and at all other times drew pictures of engines both large and small, with the assistance of a squeaky slate-pencil and curling tongue, much to the admiration of the rest of the small-fry." Hall was not exactly a model student, and while he took a stray course or two later, he never received a high school, much less college, diploma. This hardly made for an auspicious-looking launch to a long and influential engineering career. But Hall was blessed with a remarkable intellect, and that mattered more at the time than possessing a diploma. He left home early, too, displaying a restlessness seen his entire life. While still a teenager, Hall boarded with a baker for $5 per week, lured inside the establishment because he saw an engine inside an adjacent front door. And while Elbert baked, he continued drawing engines. Even as a young man E.J. Hall exhibited an irrepressible attraction to engines, which provided the energy needed for a remarkable career trajectory.

As the 19th century closed, Hall effortlessly transitioned from drawing engines to designing them. For one local employer he rebuilt gasoline engines, which brought him to the attention of San Francisco-based I.L. Burton in 1901. There he designed a line of small engines including a stationary model called the "Doak," which became popular with farmers. Amply proving himself, in 1902 the 20-year-old became half-owner in Burton, an establishment that served as both employer and classroom.

With the stunning flurry of advances made in automotive and aviation circles around the turn of the 20th century, it's little wonder that the engine-consumed Hall gravitated in that direction, as had figures like Clessie Cummins, Jesse Vincent, Ransom Olds and Henry Ford. Hall's introduction to automotive work came in 1905 when he joined the tiny Heine-Velox auto venture of San Francisco. According to Kevin

Above: In his business operations, as in this Heine-Velox automobile, the headstrong Gustav Heine was in the driver's seat, and Elbert Hall was in the passenger's seat. Below: A Comet newspaper ad, judging from the Hall-Kennedy name, from 1908-09.

Tikker, "Hall functioned variously as works driver, repairman, chauffeur, salesmen[sic], and general partner" at Heine-Velox. It is unclear how much Hall influenced engineering there, but Heine-Velox autos were fast, powerful and cleverly designed. The April 1906 earthquake terminated his job but not Hall's passion in autos; he was hooked.

As Hall honed his engineering skills, he also acquired a love for auto racing, both as a driver and a mechanic. It was exciting, fun, and a means to test ideas. Years later Hall's widow wrote that "before 1910 all automobile racers in the Bay region were bringing their cars to his shop to be improved or repaired." While he never became a serious race-car driver, Hall was a member of a team that broke a record driving from San Francisco to Los Angeles in November 1906 (18 hours, 13 minutes) in a Columbia. Putting aside breaking records, in 1907 Hall returned to San Jose to work at Occidental Motor Car Company. There remains some confusion about Hall's duties at Occidental because under its roof several different

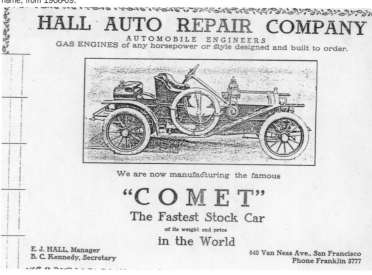

HALL AUTO REPAIR COMPANY
AUTOMOBILE ENGINEERS
GAS ENGINES of any horsepower or style designed and built to order.

We are now manufacturing the famous

"COMET"
The Fastest Stock Car
of its weight and price
in the World

E. J. HALL, Manager
B. C. Kennedy, Secretary

640 Van Ness Ave., San Francisco
Phone Franklin 3777

cars, such as the locally popular Sunset, were produced. It is certain, however, that while at Occidental Hall built his own first automobile, the Comet.

Fast, nimble and small, Hall's Comet lived up to its celestial name. It rode on a 102-inch wheelbase, powered by a Hall-designed 201-cubic-inch, overhead-valve, 4-cylinder engine that produced 25 horsepower. Although not sounding impressive, those 25 horse-

amazing achievement, especially from an individual lacking significant financial backing. While not the first V8 built in America, the engine was highly unusual nonetheless, ahead of its time. The most widely publicized application of Hall's V8 was in Peter English's "Helicopter," an ill-fated experimental craft. Even if he was not becoming a household name, Hall was gaining the attention of car makers, aviators, and engineers as a man on the cutting edge of engine-making.

A Serendipitous Meeting

In 1908, Bert Carlise Scott, son of a northern California business magnate, visited Hall's shop. Scott had just purchased an Autocar and wanted the renowned Hall to inspect it. While going over the Autocar, Hall suggested the two men go for a spin in one of his Comets. Even 48 years later Scott vividly remembered the meeting, writing: "I recall going up

Above: Hall and Scott's first product, finished in 1909. Below: The engine compartment of the fifth Hall-Scott motor car, built for Nevada Copper Belt and delivered in 1911, with a six-cylinder, 150hp Hall-Scott engine.

power moved the Comet in impressive fashion. At a 1908 race the Comet so dominated the field, winning seven of eight events it entered, race promoters barred it from further competition. As reported in *Motor Age*, the Comet, which had a "body that is a mere miniature, a veritable toy ... passed" at will Autocars, Buicks, Maxwells and "even the powerful Stearns." Before retiring from the race the Comet set a West Coast speed record. Bucking convention, Hall opted for achieving greater efficiency through sophistication over brutish displacement. Although barely remembered today, the Comet pointed the way for future engine development.

Racing success does not always lead to abundant auto sales, and Comet production halted when Occidental closed its doors in 1907. Perhaps Hall never bothered taking his possessions out of boxes during the early 20th century. That same year he moved back to San Francisco, where he built a few more Comets and engines at Hall's Auto Repair and then Hall-Kennedy Engineering. Always pushing himself to greater achievement, around 1908 Hall began selling a 60hp V8, an

Powell Street from a standing start at Sutter Street, and exceeding 40 mph when we reached the top of the grade at California Street." Greatly impressed, Scott ordered a Comet for himself and convinced two of his friends to do the same. With that test drive the two men formed a long business and personal relationship.

Sensing Hall's considerable engineering talents, Scott proposed that the two men build a motorized rail car, a "motor car." Scott's father was a partner in the Yreka Railroad where Bert had served as secretary. Bert was thus familiar with existing motor cars, found them wanting, and believed Hall could build a superior one. Hall agreed to join forces with Scott and do just that. Scott arranged with San Francisco railcar maker Holman and Company to build the body and trucks while Hall tackled the running gear. According to Scott, "Hall designed and built in his shop a four cylinder, valve-in-head engine, 8-inch bore, 10-inch stroke, a two-piece circular band clutch, propeller shaft drive [mated to a] four-speed gear box." More impressive than Hall's 2,010-cubic-inch engine might have

The Old Rhineback Aerodrome in Rhineback, N.Y., probably has the last Hall-Scott engine powering an airplane, shown here. The restored V8 engine below was used to power a Curtiss Model D Pusher piloted by Old Rhineback Aerodrome pilot Dan Taylor.

been his clever transmission, which he built having four ratios either forward or backward, available by simply shifting a lever. At that time, rail motor car and auto technology were very similar, as were auto and aviation, so there was considerable technology transfer between them.

After three months Hall and Holman finished their work. According to Scott, the rail company found the car "very satisfactory, supplanting steam locomotive operation, and the savings offset cost of the car within a few years." Flush with success, the two decided to build more such vehicles and in 1910 formed the Hall-Scott Motor Car Company, named after their *reason d'être* – building rail motor cars. They erected a factory in Berkeley and a business office across the bay in San Francisco. Scott, the college grad, handled business affairs while Hall, the self-educated engineer, designed the company's products. Over the next few years Hall designed more rail engines and a variety of other rail cars, but the number produced remained quite small; Hall was focusing his talents elsewhere.

Left: The V8 "Special Car" owned by Leland Scott, Bert's younger brother. It is possible that the Special Car was the Hall V8-powered auto that Cadillac engineers purchased to study when designing their own V8.

CREATIVITY IN MOTION

The 1910s were exciting years at Hall-Scott, and it was in aviation where E.J. Hall and Hall-Scott gained national and international recognition. The company carried over Hall's in-line 4-cylinder and V8 engines, and he developed new ones for the flying market. They all used "built-up" (also known as "separate cylinder") design, where each cylinder was individually cast and bolted to the crankcase. They also used interchangeable parts, which allowed the small company to maximize the number of models marketed by varying number of cylinders, stroke, bore, carburetion, etc., while minimizing the variety of bits peculiar to each. Thus, the A-1 (the 4-cylinder) and A-2 (the eight) used the same cylinder barrels, valve train, and so forth. And the engines used overhead valves, two per cylinder, actuated by pushrods and rocker arms, a rarity among engines at the time but common today. As with every Hall-Scott ever built, the A-1 and A-2 were water cooled, having water jackets pressed to the cylinders and coolant passages bored into the heads. They both employed force-fed oil lubrication, a must for aircraft engines. Hall-Scott soon fol-

lowed with two more related V8s, quickly becoming a leading aviation power provider.

In spite of Hall's love of and experience with autos, Hall-Scott engines powered few automobiles, but a couple of cars with Hall engines have received attention from historians and auto aficionados. Bert Scott's brother Leland owned a custom-made vehicle, referred to by the Scott family as the "Special Car," which had a one-off Hall-built V8. In fact, D. McCall White, Wilfred Leland, Charles "Boss" Kettering and Edward Deeds of Delco Labs studied it when they developed Cadillac's famous V8. Bert's nephew Leland Jr. recounted how Hall, in a discussion with Kettering, a longtime friend of E.J., suggested, "'Why not get something really new and different like an 8-cylinder engine.' Kettering said, 'Who in the world has an eight cylinder?' 'Well,' said Hall, 'Lee Scott out in California has one I designed for him.'"

Kettering called Scott and agreed to buy his Special Car for $5,000. "Fine," said Kettering, "put it on a freight and send it in all haste to me." Scott did not sell Kettering a production Hall-Scott V8, though, as Hall informed Cadillac engineer C.F. Arnold in a 1954 letter: "It was 4-inch bore and 4-inch stroke," Hall

recalled. "The crankshaft, connecting rods and pistons were from one of our standard aviation engines. The rest of the entire engine was built up special and had a number of unique features for the time." Some of these special touches included water-jacketed exhaust manifolds, spark plug wires covered by aluminum covers, and "cylinder blocks [that] were [cast] in pairs without cylinder heads and were held down by four through bolts which extended through and took care of securing the rocker arm covers."

Cadillac engineers tore down and studied the Hall engine. Little surprise, the V8 they built, which earned considerable acclaim, shared some features of the Hall V8. The two V8s had cylinders with 90-degree banks and cylinders cast in pairs, although the Cadillac displaced 314 cubic inches, had an L-head, and used integrally cast coolant passages. Hall influenced Cadillac in building a V8, even if Cadillac did not build a Hall engine.

A second example, the Hall-Scott-powered 1917 Fageol, was simply outrageous. Truck, tractor and bus maker Fageol boasted that it was the most expensive car built in America at more than $12,000, and it used a six-cylinder Hall-Scott aviation engine. Sadly, only a handful of these very expensive, fast and sophisticated machines were produced before war restrictions curtailed production. Hall's talents were gaining attention.

To point, with their industry-leading performance, Hall-Scott engines quickly earned plenty of flattering press. In 1910, *Cycle and Automotive Trade Journal* reported: "The designer of these motors is E. J. Hall, who is well known on the coast as the designer of the 'Comet' automobile which was very successful in making numerous track records." Barnstormers, trick flyers of the period, including well-known figures like Thomas Baldwin, Charles Walsh and H.F. Kearny, often flew with Hall-Scotts. An author of the time noted, "Originally the majority of aircraft motors came from France and the cost … was prohibitive for the average experimenter." But Hall-Scott engines, which

A-5 was an early example of the overhead cam and hemi, not to mention an aluminum crankcase. These features became fixtures on all Hall-Scott engines, regardless of application or size, decades before they began to creep slowly into wider acceptance. With this engine, Hall became recognized as a design leader, especially with heads and valvetrain.

Following the A-5, Hall-Scott released the A-7, which had aluminum pistons in addition to the features seen in the A-5. The A-7 was quite sophisticated, making it sound modern even a hundred years later. Hall then bored the A-7's four cylinders to 5.25 inches to create the A-7a. The potent A-7a boasted an impressive power-to-weight ratio of 3.81 pounds per horsepower. It was in aviation where Hall applied most of his creative genius in this period.

WARTIME DEMAND

World War I had a huge impact on many American firms and individuals, and Hall-Scott and E.J. Hall were no different. During the conflict Hall-Scott found the United States and a number of foreign governments eager to purchase its engines; Russia alone ordered 300 A-5s. In May 1917, a month after Congress declared war against the Central Powers, Hall-Scott tested its A-8, the company's first V-12, which was capable of moving a much bigger airplane than its existing engines. The V-12 had a bore and stroke of 5 x 7 inches, produced more than 300 horsepower and was Hall's most impressive engine achievement to date. Hall joined the military in 1917 to help the war effort, rising to the rank of lieutenant colonel.

The federal government had some very specific plans for Hall and his company during the war. The Aircraft Production Board had been formed to build a winning Allied aircraft engine design. On the board was Edward Deeds of Delco Labs, a man familiar with Hall's skill. According to F.E. Mosckovics, who sat in some of the group's initial meetings, Deeds invited Hall to the project in spring 1917, assembling what Moscovics called a meeting "between the two best-posted men in America on aircraft matters. Lt. Col. E.J. Hall, who actually had more aerial motor experience than any other American engineer, and Lt. Col. J.G. Vincent, than whom no one in this country had more experience on the details of the Mercedes-type air motors."

Sounding more like lore than fact, Hall, Vincent and helpers sequestered themselves in the Willard Hotel in Washington, D.C., in late May 1917. After five days of round-the-clock work they emerged with a design. It was a success, and by the holiday season of 1918 quantity production of "Liberty Motors" began at several automakers. Hall-Scott provided dies for some Liberty parts, but did not produce any of the engines, contrary to common misperceptions, which Hall-Scott did nothing to correct.

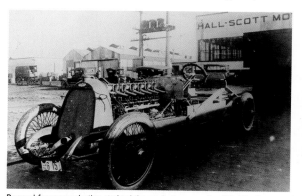

Demand for war production strained the production capacity of Hall-Scott, preventing it from supplying nearby Fageol with A-5s for its autos in 1917. Shown here is the potent Fageol in bare chassis and with its body intact. Below right: Daredevil Glenn Martin in 1911 with a Hall-Scott V8-powered plane.

were "unusually powerful in relation to their weight and what was more important they were reliable," appeared, "and soon a Hall-Scott motor was the ambition of every early experimenter." While many tried to break into the aviation engine market in the 1910s, Hall-Scott became a leader.

In 1915, Hall-Scott released its first 6-cylinder aviation engine, the A-5. Hall fitted the A-5 with an overhead camshaft, which actuated the two valves in each cylinder. The valves were inclined because, for improved combustion, the A-5 had domed, or hemispherical, combustion chambers – "hemi" heads. The

Hall-Scott workers standing around an A-5 powerplant with some of the more significant features of the engine visible here.

The Liberty was a remarkable achievement, especially given its rushed development. Hall and Vincent designed a family of related engines of four, six, eight and 12 cylinders using interchangeable parts, so models used the same pistons, cylinders and valves. All shared a bore and stroke of 5 x 7 inches. Liberties used built-up design, overhead camshaft, hemi head, aluminum crankcase and pistons, and pressed-steel water jackets. In other words, the Liberty looked a lot like Hall-Scott's A-5, A-7 and A-8. Liberties were not identical to Hall-Scotts, but Hall's signature was abundantly evident nonetheless.

E.J. Hall worked with engineers from across the auto industry to insure efficient allied aviation production. In early 1918, Hall began consulting on the French Le Rhone engine and British DeHaviland and Bristol airplanes. To expedite greater European air-power production, in July 1918 he sailed across the Atlantic to become Chief of the Technical Section, Air Service, American Expeditionary Force. America's swift mobilization soon broke the war's stalemate, leading to Germany's request for peace in November 1918. His mission accomplished, Hall received an honorable discharge, and for his amazing efforts, the Distinguished Service Medal. Liberties played their part in the victory, powering planes credited with more than 60 "kills."

Writers heralded the Liberty, then and in the decades since. The *San Francisco Examiner* crowed that "a portion of the credit for the celebrated new 'Liberty Motor,' said to be the fastest and finest airplane motor in the world, is claimed by Berkeley, inasmuch as E. J. Hall of the Hall-Scott Motor Car Company of that city

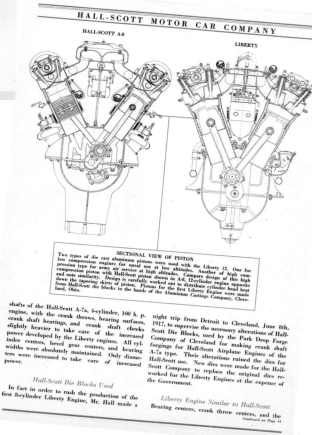

Top: The V-12 Liberty.
Above: Explaining the Hall-Scott connection to the famous engine.

had a hand in designing it." In his 1920 book *The Story of the Engine*, author Wilbur Decker wrote that the Liberty was "the crowning example in mechanical achievement." For years after the war, Liberties powered a few fast cars, record-breaking speedboats, and

even tanks. More recently, Philip Dickey wrote that "Liberty design was a complete departure" from most leading aircraft engines of its day. Hall was justifiably proud of his wartime accomplishments.

War did nothing to squelch Hall's love of designing, building and tinkering. Said John E. "Speed" Glidewell, longtime Hall friend, employee, and fellow engineer, "When there was a new experimental engine on the dynamometer he would get fidgety and anxious to see it go. He'd sometimes get impatient and yank the throttle open – maybe she'd stick up, and if so he'd have a bit of a sheepish grin on and tell the guys to fix 'er and we'll try it again. He was not what you would call a tough task master but he knew what he wanted … and was 'at it' all hours of the day." His approach to work seemed natural and intuitive. Said a man who worked under him in war and peacetime, Harold Hicks, "Hall was not a graduate engineer, but he is a man who had had so much design experience that he could almost accurately guess the sizes of things as he laid them out. Of course, he was a very brilliant man; that is, he was shrewd. He was a good designer. He didn't actually get on the board and make a design himself because his draftmanship was rather crude." The boy who spent his school years consumed by drawing engines could still be seen in the adult E.J. Hall.

ENGINE MASTERY

The post-WWI years brought a great many changes in the work of Hall. He consulted at Buick on engine and rear axle development. He teamed with engineers at International Harvester and created two popular heavy-duty, 4-cylinder truck engines. He managed to continue his association with auto racers like Ed Cooper, Ralph DePalma and Glover Ruckstell, although there is no evidence of Hall auto racing after the war. These men often built and tested cars or components at Hall-Scott or Hall's home, and Hall was called upon to fine-tune valvetrain, cylinder head and camshaft problems.

In November 1920, Hall wrote to Pliny Holt of Holt

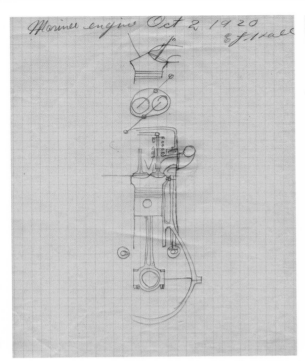

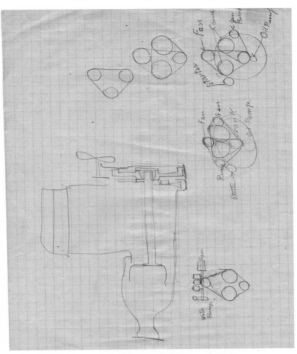

Above: E.J. Hall's handwritten notes for a marine engine. Below: The Holt T-35 tractor was popular, with more than 10,000 eventually built through 1928.

Hall spent most of his postwar consulting time at Ford Motor Company. Henry Ford was a great admirer of Hall as an engineer and a man. Like Hall, Ford was a mechanical genius and self-taught engineer, which the auto titan respected greatly. Ford brought Hall to Michigan in 1919 for several projects, including helping with his struggle over what kind of trolley system would be used in Detroit – electric with overhead wires or gasoline-powered. For Ford's gasoline-powered trolley Hall built an in-line 4-cylinder engine, turned it 90 degrees on its side, and placed it under the floor between the frame rails. In one car he even coupled together two of the engines. The engines had some familiar Hall touches, such as 5 x 7-inch bore and stroke, and the ability to power the car as fast forward or backward. Harold Hicks, who had served with Hall in WWI and then at Ford, wrote: "The reverse was an idea Colonel Hall had. A little slipping dog was used in the nest of beveled gears. By throwing it in one direction, the car would go in one direction. Moving it to the other set of gears and driving through them, the car would go in the

Manufacturing, a predecessor of Caterpillar and a fellow northern California firm. Hall proposed building for Holt a lightweight, high rpm 4-cylinder motor, its cylinders cast together, "enbloc," as opposed to "built up." Holt approved the plan, so in March 1921 the two companies signed the first of three contracts for Hall-Scott to build hundreds of engines for the new small T-35 (later known as the Two-Ton) tractor. The Holt powerplant was Hall-Scott's first enbloc engine, and mastering this design allowed the company to serve many other segments of the industrial engine market. These new markets included buses, with another northern California vehicle builder, Fageol, asking Hall-Scott to modify the Holt engine to power its trend-setting new Safety Coach. Wrote a reviewer in *The Motor Truck* about the popular vehicle, "Among the several powerplants that this writer has seen, none is superior to the Hall-Scott, an engine designed by Col. E.J. Hall, one of the designers of the Liberty Aeroplane Engine." Hall and Hall-Scott remained linked to the touted Liberty motor for decades.

opposite direction. It was very ingenious."

Design, building and testing shot ahead in typical Hall fashion. Although the car ran well (and so smoothly that a supervisor who stood over the running engine asked, "Say, where are the engines in this car?"), its costs did not justify choosing it over electricity, so Ford lost the fight. Still, Hall learned lessons at Ford that he took back to Berkeley and later applied to powering buses.

For a great many years the Ford name was synonymous with its iconic Model T. Justifiably reluctant to tamper with that success, Henry Ford nonetheless charged Hall with the risky task of re-powering it. Given the affordable price of the Model T, Hall had to design a different kind of motor than he had designed for Hall-Scott. This did not pose a problem for the skilled engineer. Hall-Scott personnel assembled several "Little Six" engines in Berkeley, and Hall omitted costly features in them such as widespread use of aluminum or an overhead camshaft, opting instead for a lower cost "L-head." His respect for Hall notwithstanding, after a small number had been fitted into cars for testing Henry Ford scuttled the Little Six for reasons unknown, but probably relating to cost.

Henry Ford also supported Hall through his approval of a Hall-Scott-built item for the Model T. In 1921 another wartime associate of Hall, Glover Ruckstell, brought a two-speed rear axle to Hall-Scott for manufacture. Hall-Scott staff and Hall's racing buddy, Harry Miller, performed considerable work on the component and then released it as the Ruckstell Axle. Hall's wife later observed that "due to its excellent service and the great confidence that Mr. Ford had in my husband's talent, the Ford Company then consented to allow the

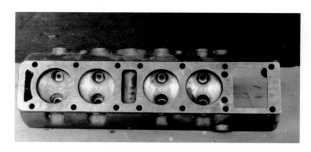

Ford dealers to sell it," a rare practice. Through 1925, Hall-Scott made more than 200,000 Ruckstell Axles, then turned over production to Eaton, which continued and expanded the operation. Hall consulted for Ford in the years ahead, and even sold Henry's son Edsel his Hall-Scott-powered speedboat, so he appears to have remained in the Ford family's good graces.

In the 1920s at Hall-Scott, Hall designed a number

Above: Fageol used hundreds of Hall-Scott engines to power its coaches, such as this Safety Coach, in the 1920s. Top: Visible here is the hemispherical or "hemi" head, a Hall signature design feature, used in the T-35's engine. Right: Easy to install and inexpensive, the Ruckstell Axle dramatically improved Model T performance by providing four forward and two reverse gears.

gasified fuels: propane, butane and liquefied petroleum gas (LPG). ACF buses began using LPG-fueled Hall-Scotts around 1930. Applying lessons from Ford, Hall-Scott began providing horizontal engines for ACF buses in the early 1930s.

But Hall's crowning achievement in this period was designing the Invader. This 998-cubic-inch, 6-cylinder marine engine was powerful, efficient and sleek; most models produced between 250 and 275 horsepower. One magazine gushed over the new powerplant in 1931, calling it "light in weight (1,800 to 1,900 pounds) due to its extremely compact and neat design, and is sturdy and strong," and "the results have been astonishingly good." Numerous sources report that during the later years of Prohibition, "rum runners"

Top: Often recognized as the first international airmail delivery, this Hall-Scott L-4-powered Boeing made history in 1919. Above left: Hall-Scott's LM engines won a number of high-profile races, lending a certain panache seen in this ad. Above right: Hall sold this Hall-Scott-powered boat to Edsel Ford. Hall often wore a suit and tie even while at leisure. Right: Hall-Scott truck and bus engines won wide recognition for their great pulling power, and company ads promoted power, as seen here.

of interesting engines, bristling with new features and ever-better performance. Engineering at Hall-Scott changed in 1925 when rail car and bus maker American Car and Foundry (ACF) purchased the Berkeley engine company, giving Hall and Hall-Scott a degree of stability. His new models ranged in size from the 377-cubic-inch, 6-cylinder Model 95 horizontal bus engine to the 2,386-cubic-inch, 6-cylinder Model 350 (and 357) industrial engine for boats, trains and pumps. The LM-6, a Liberty-based marine engine, powered award-winning speedboats and was perhaps the first engine built using full-flow oil filtration (accomplished with lubrication leader Charles Winslow). Hall and staff engineers tinkered with

were common Invader buyers, using the big Hall-Scotts to outrun lawmen when spiriting alcohol into the United States. The Invader was the last all-new engine he designed for the firm.

Above: Hall on the left and Norman DeVaux on the right, with the ill-timed 6-75. Right: Citroën's Traction Avant was the first mass-produced front-wheel-drive car with a monocoque chassis and hydraulic brakes. Hall worked at Citroën during perhaps that company's most exciting period.

Auto Focus

By the opening of the new decade it appeared the prolific engineer needed a change. In June 1930, Norman DeVaux, an auto salesman and executive, proposed that he and Hall build automobiles. According to company literature, "Typical of the manner in which Col. Hall acts, he accepted, almost immediately." Several sources around Hall noted that he had grown weary of dealing with ACF management, so Hall accepted DeVaux's invitation, left Hall-Scott, and formed the DeVaux-Hall Motors Company. The ever-optimistic DeVaux believed that the nation's economic problems would be short-lived. Besides, there would always be demand for an attractively priced car giving buyers excellent value for their dollar, and that was exactly how he marketed the DeVaux car.

The new car hit the showrooms amazingly soon, late January 1931, because the DeVaux 6-75 was closely based on an existing car, the Durant. The engine used in

the 6-75 was not all-new either. Hall refined the engine with help from engine-maker Continental, which also built it. The 6-75's engine – a 65-70hp, L-head, 6-cylinder – did not look like a Hall-Scott. "Flatheads" are reliable, smooth and cheap to manufacture; low cost was a particular plus in those Depression years. Hall coaxed more power from Conti's A-22 engine with changes to carburetion, ignition and manifolds, resulting in surprising performance.

The undeniable talent of the two founders was not enough to bring DeVaux-Hall success, however. After considerable initial hoopla (and a million dollars spent on advertising), glowing press, sharp styling and exceptional performance for its price, sales sputtered. In early 1932, the poorly capitalized company slipped into receivership, just over a year after beginning production. Creditor Continental, unable to recover money owed it, purchased DeVaux-Hall, renamed and reworked the car, produced a couple thousand examples, but in 1934 threw in the towel as well. E.J. Hall was already long gone by then.

Wasting little time after the mercifully quick demise of DeVaux-Hall, Hall moved to France in 1932 to work at Citroën. Hall not only engineered cars at Citroën but also made changes in personnel and plant organization. André Citroën and Henry Ford were friends; in fact, Hall's move to France followed on the heels of a trip Citroën made to America. One can easily imagine the supportive Ford endorsing the services of Hall to the French automaker. The mid-1930s were exciting years at Citroën, with new models brimming with bold technology, like front-wheel drive (*Traction Avant*) and monocoque bodies. But André Citroën died in 1935 and talk of war swept Europe, prompting Hall's return to California. Hall's brief tenure at Citroën was fruitful but was his last serious stint with automotive engineering.

END OF A PROLIFERATE CAREER

Upon his return to the States, Hall jumped between positions, which included consulting, engineering and management. Hall spent most of the war years working at a laboratory in Glendale, Calif., which he opened in 1942. Hall's genius was so broad that, according to one report, he designed "several important electronic devices, including noise suppressor circuits for radios, for receivers in airport control towers, and for radio direction finders; static suppresser circuits for airplane compasses; and an electronic relay receiving clear continuous wave or code through the heaviest noise conditions or radar at exceptionally high speed."

With the war over, Hall shifted gears again and in

Left: The scale of the components and the close tolerances demanded in the wind tunnel projects Hall worked on while at Westinghouse was daunting. Above: Hall, standing at far right, late in his life at a Westinghouse retirement party. The other two men are unidentified. Below: Although not usually noted for his work with diesels, Hall helped Joshua Hendy with the introduction of such engines after WWII, as diesels grabbed increasing market share in heavy-duty applications.

1946 joined the Joshua Hendy Iron Works near San Jose, at first helping to introduce two new industrial diesels. When Westinghouse bought Hendy shortly after his arrival, his new employer put Hall on another project far from automotive engineering – wind tunnels. Westinghouse undertook several similar massive projects in those years, including some of the largest in the world, and Hall, now of retirement age, was front and center in their development.

During his Westinghouse years Hall began to curtail his workload and ease into semi-retirement. His mind

Fig. A. Hendy Stationary Diesel Engine

never slowed, however; he even proposed a new swimming cap design to a rubber company. But after several years of declining health, in October 1955 at the age of 73, Hall died at his home in Los Gatos, Calif. The obituary in the *San Jose Mercury News* described Hall as "one of the most renowned engineers in the United States," the man who "during World War I designed the famed Liberty aircraft engine based on the 'A-5-A' which he developed in 1915."

Hall was indeed accomplished, but he has received curiously little recognition, perhaps because he spent little time on self-promotion. Hall's designs remain his chief legacy, even if his name never achieved the deserved recognition. Hall is an excellent example, among the last, of an earlier era in automotive history when the leading edge of technology was pushed forward by figures lacking university degrees and heavy corporate capitalization. More than a century after Hall's birth, the automotive world still moves on rubber tires powered by piston engines burning petroleum-based fuels, but the engineers who create this technology have radically different training. AQ

Rally for the Ages

The 1968 London-Sydney Marathon

Adventure – it's like a magnet to many people. Such was the attraction when news of a motoring event that would have car crews driving almost nonstop from London to Sydney leaked to the media. It was too much of a challenge to resist, and nominations for the inaugural London-Sydney Marathon to be held at the end of 1968 poured in. Soon the organizers had more than 150 cars and teams ready to go.

BY GAVIN FARMER

What set the huge event in motion was nothing more romantic than a lunchtime chat over a few beers by some editorial executives at the *Daily Express* in London. They were kicking some ideas around, ideas that would generate publicity for their publishing group and at the same time fire the public's imagination. Why not a motoring marathon? Surely the various car manufacturers would be keen to support such an event and the publicity it would generate would be enormous. So it seemed, although conspicuous by their absence were the Japanese manufacturers.

Two dynamic businessmen were the key to mov-

Left: Keith Schellenberg's Bentley touring sports in London. Above: Barry Ferguson speeds past Mt. Ararat. Below: The two-wheel-drive Land Rover of the 17-21 Lancers.

ing it from concept to reality. Both were tough and unyielding and had created huge and vastly profitable media empires. They were Sir Max Aitken, chairman of the Beaverbrook Group of Companies and publisher of the *Daily Express*; and Sir Frank Packer, chairman and managing director of Australian Consolidated Press, publisher of the Sydney *Daily Telegraph*. Following some discussions the two men

agreed to cosponsor the event and offered a £10,000 prize to the winner. Cars could be entered singularly or if a manufacturer entered three cars as a team. As in normal rallies, points would be lost for lateness into a designated control point, with the car that has lost the least points being the winner. An organizing commit-

tee was established to get the marathon on the road; it would be the greatest motoring event since the Peking-Paris epic of 1907.

Englishman Jack Sears, former race and rally driver, was appointed event organizer. He and his team set about planning the route and discussing the event with the appropriate people in the governments of the many countries through which the cars would pass. The event would run from London, across France and into Italy, then into the eastern bloc countries of Yugoslavia and Bulgaria before crossing the Bosphorus at Istanbul, on across Turkey, Afghanistan, West Pakistan (as it was then known) to Bombay (today Mumbai) in India before shipping the surviving cars to Fremantle for the dash across Australia.

In the event, 98 cars were to start, comprising 43 different models of car from 15 countries that included

Below: The Australian contingent (left to right): R. Forsyth, B. Hodgson, G. Hoinville, Miss World Penny Plummer, D. Rutherford, J. Ellis, J. Gowland, I. Vaughan.

a crew driving a 1930 Bentley Sports Tourer. The most popular single model was the Austin 1800 Mk II – nicknamed the "Land Crab" by the rally fraternity, it was strong but slow – with 10 entered. The factory entered five 1800 Mk IIs for ace drivers including Paddy Hopkirk, Ruano Aaltonen and Timo Makinen with renowned long-distance expert Evan Green leading a crew from BMC Australia.

Eight English Ford Cortinas were entered, most of which were Lotus-Cortinas (four factory cars with Englishman Roger Clark as their lead driver). Five Porsche 911s (lead driver was the Polish ace Sobieslaw Zasada) were on the list, as was a motley assortment of cars. Entrants ranged from a Volvo 145 station wagon entered by Miss Elsie Gadd and her three-woman crew; a Chrysler Valiant wagon entered by Phil Lumsden; a Rambler American for Sidney Dickson; and specialist tuner Jeff Uren entered a Ford Savage V6. The Dutch National Team entered two DAF 55 sedans that amazingly finished. Ford of Germany and Ford of Australia entered three cars each – Taunus 20M RS for the Germans with Dieter Glemser, "Jochi" Kleint and Simo Lampinen driving, and big Falcon GTs for the Aussies, who included Harry "The Fox" Firth and Ian Vaughan driving. Avtoexport in Moscow entered four Moskvich 408 sedans, all of which finished.

Chrysler's French subsidiary Simca entered four of their new 1100 hatchback model while the Rootes Group, Chrysler's English problem child and a major rally competitor, prepared a Hillman Hunter for Scottish ace Andrew Cowan. The Sydney *Daily Telegraph* entered four cars under its banner: three were V8-powered Holden Monaro GTS coupes with 350 cid, Turboglide automatic transmission and air conditioning, and the fourth was a Morris 1100 crewed by three women who were employees of the newspaper. Although they lost 8,111 points, they also surprisingly finished. Citroën, big in rallies in Europe, entered only two factory cars – one for Lucien Bianchi, the other for Robert Neyret – that were supported by the various Citroën car clubs along the route.

RALLY REASONING

The philosophies of the various team managers responsible for the preparation of the cars were interesting. Bill Barnett from Ford's facility at Boreham said, "We knew we had to strengthen the body because the terrain we had surveyed told us the cars would take a hammering, but we left the engine and running gear pretty much as it was for ease of servicing along the way." Jochen Neerpasch from Ford Cologne had much the same idea insofar as the Taunuses were bodily strengthened and the engines tuned to cope with the varying qualities of fuel they would have to use.

John Gowland, team manager from Ford Australia commented, "The Ford UK and Germany guys made all kinds of snide comments about the 'trucks' as they called the Falcons. To them our cars were far too big and heavy and nowhere near sophisticated enough. They couldn't understand that we were driving in a marathon, not a 48-hour sprint rally! When we think about it now their cars were more race-prepared than

rally prepared, silly really.

"We detuned the 302 cid V8 but still had 200-plus bhp and the cars could easily cruise at 120-125mph. Apart from seam welding the body, we did not have to modify it at all. It was already a strong car."

At Rootes, manager Des O'Dell and lead driver Cowan collaborated to build an extremely robust car. "We were not in the same league as the big teams so we had to be smarter. We built and tested the Hunter (the only Rootes Group car suited to the event) at Bagshot, which is a tank testing ground. I knew when we'd finished our development, typically belt-and-braces stuff, that we had a car capable of withstanding the punishment," Cowan told the author.

Peter Browning, competitions manager at British Leyland, prepared the four factory team cars at the MG works at Abingdon. The bodies were strengthened by seam welding and the installation of a rollover bar at the B-pillar, a 'roo bar replaced the front bumper and each mechanical component was carefully balanced and reassembled. Extra lights were fitted and the spare

Above: Paddy Hopkirk somewhere in the Great Australian Outback. Below: One of the Russian Moskvich 408s kicking up dust in rural Australia.

tires were carried on the roof. Unlike their rivals at Ford, BLMC chose to enhance the performance of the engines to cope with the 1800 Mk II's weight. Having said that, Evan Green said of his car, "It was a tank that downhill could be coaxed up to 90 mph. Its redeeming feature was that it was a very, very strong car in which I had ultimate faith."

It was much the same with the preparation of every car entered: how to make it stronger without incurring

machine. Preparations would be vital to the success or otherwise of the teams.

Dunlop, BP and Castrol soon found themselves inundated with requests for sponsorship following the announcement. They did what any British company would have done: embrace the marathon and as many of the competitors as possible and support them with products and assistance for the whole event.

The major factory-backed teams were able to carry

rest of us flew to London, picked up two Mark IV V6 Zephyrs and drove the London-to-Istanbul section where we met up with the other two and along the way we collected the various currencies we'd need."

The biggest issue facing all teams was the logistics of service and spare parts backup across some of the most desolate areas of the world. As Bill Barnett and John Gowland from Ford commented, "Through our industry contacts we were able to get fuel reserves set up across the whole route. For spare parts we made up packages – hoses, tie rod ends, wheel bearings, those kinds of things – and had them dispatched to various locations along the way. India was a special problem for us because we were not allowed to send parts there." Luck smiled on them through the agency of the Ford Foundation of India that had Australian XT Falcons on the fleet and as Gowland wryly added: "It was our corporate responsibility to keep them supplied with parts!"

The highest placed Holden Monaro driver, Barry Ferguson, powers through the outback.

THE ADVENTURE BEGINS

The first car to be flagged off at 1400 hours on Sunday, Nov. 24, by Desmond Plummer, chairman of the Greater London Council, with TV commentary by Raymond Baxter, was the Ford Cortina GT of Bill Bengry. The second car was flagged off by reigning Miss World, Penny Plummer from Australia, and that was the Harry Firth Ford Falcon GT. The rest of the starters were flagged off at one-minute intervals, cheered on by more than 20,000 people who had crowded into Crystal Palace.

Stage one was the 728-mile run to Turin via Paris in 25 hours, 52 minutes. The French authorities had banned the cars from the autoroutes, which meant that crews had to navigate the French B roads at night in thick fog. Not an auspicious start. Rumor had it that some crews used the autoroutes but covered up their numbers. Crews were also promised a motorcycle escort out of Paris, a huge and poorly signposted city, but this failed to materialize. Once out of Paris the cars raced south across the Alps through the Mount Blanc tunnel to Turin.

too much of a weight penalty and at the same time have sufficient power to maintain the required average speeds. After all, the marathon would cover many extremes of geography, altitude, temperature and road conditions, from the fast autostradas in Italy to rough dirt tracks in the Australian desert and everything in between. It would be a severe test of both man and

out their own reconnaissance, but to assist the others Castrol announced that they were going to provide each team with route notes. Ford, for example, surveyed the roads from London to Bombay in a Lotus-Cortina that the Australians Hodgson and Rutherford picked up when they flew to Bombay and set out to survey the route in reverse. Graham Hoinville: "The

From there they headed towards Istanbul via Belgrade, a drive of 1,300 miles for which the teams were allowed 36 hours, 43 minutes. With the good roads and the high speeds, this section proved to be a simple affair for most and allowed the crews some rest in Belgrade. One of the fancied Ford cars crewed by Soderstrom and Palm broke a timing chain in this section and lost an enormous amount of time finding a replacement. Near Venice the Harper/Pollard Ford experienced water pump troubles and one of the two Vauxhall Ventoras retired after a crash. As Ford UK team driver Nick Brittain observed in his book *Marathon: Around the World in a Cloud of Dust*, "We left Italy without any fanfare at all. Frankly we were surprised by the Italians who are generally speed-crazy, car-happy loons but they were unimpressed with the passage of the marathon cars. The Yugoslavs were much more enthusiastic."

In the mountainous Ljubljana area, the teams experienced cold, rain and sleet for the first time. But, as Firth, Vaughan and Rutherford from the Ford Australia team said, "It wasn't wet enough to slow us down much, if at all."

At the border crossing with Bulgaria, all the crews were greeted by the authorities, who handed each car a road and weather report (in English) as well as a leather-bound diary for each crew member and some fresh apples and pears. Cowan, Firth, Brittan and others commented, "The border authorities could not have been more pleasant, it was really nice and quite different from the reception we'd got coming into France and Italy." And as Vaughan added, "Yes, and everywhere we went across Bulgaria the roads were lined with people waving to us while standing out in drizzling rain."

The inclement weather followed the cars into Turkey, where the rain increased in intensity and the winds were near gale force, this stage being a mere 547 miles in 12 hours, 25 minutes from Istanbul to Sivas in central Turkey. Several of the leading drivers were scathing of this section. Lead driver Roger Clark and many others commented: "Driving across Turkey was a nightmare. The roads were narrow and crowded with trucks, goats,

Above: Ian Vaughan, third place getter, in the Australian bush. Below: The Rover 2000 of Hemsley and Webber in the bush. They finished 37th.

cows and horses. You'd come belting around a bend and there'd be a horse and cart in the middle of the road. And the truck drivers were maniacs!"

Husband-and-wife team Nick and Jenny Brittan were eliminated here when they collided with a donkey at 80 mph and were lucky to survive with cuts and bruises.

The next stage was a short one from Sivas to Erzincan, just 175 miles away in the north of Turkey. Only two hours, 45 minutes was scheduled. Of the marathon so far, this was by far the most challenging. The section, driven at night, sorted many crews out because not only was the road narrow, it was mostly loose dirt and gravel and following a downpour, mud. All teams agreed that this section was "the hairiest" and was not helped by the fact that the rain turned to sleet and finally snow.

Vaughan: "Up in the mountains, and we were at times up around 7,000 feet above sea level, we were driving along nothing more than a track. Many teams 'came unstuck' and skidded off the road into muddy banks or off the narrow bridges. One or two even went over the edge; there was black ice everywhere because it was freezing cold."

Ford UK's top rally driver Roger Clark lost a mere six minutes through this section. David McKay driving a Monaro GTS remembered Clark's style vividly: "We were on a narrow gravel road going fairly quickly when we were passed on the outside of a bend by Clark in the Lotus-Cortina, sideways with rocks being kicked up everywhere, exhaust blaring and then in an instant he was gone into the night! It was amazing to watch him at work."

Kleint's Taunus 20M RS hurrying through the bush.

Left: Glamour girl Rosemary Smith presses on in the outback. Right: Australian veteran rally driver Ken Tubman in his Volvo 144S.

In this section Lampinen lost 14 points, Hopkirk lost 16, Glemser lost 17, Bianchi lost 18 points, as did Hodgson, Firth 20 and Evan Green 22.

In the mountains between Sivas and Erzincan, McKay slid off the road into a field and later had three studs shear off the left rear wheel. As he wrote about this misfortune: "In our hearts we knew that any chance we had of winning the marathon had just flown out of the window."

On through the night, the next stage was Teheran, 866 miles away and a time allowance of 22 hours and 1 minute – a very precise time indeed. The road wound its way up into the Elburz Mountains where there were snowstorms and it was so cold the sleet froze on the car's windscreens. At the Turkish-Iran border the authorities were quick to stamp the visas and get the teams on their way. The road in Iran was wide and bitumised so the teams could cruise easily at 90-plus mph.

However, outside Tabriz it changed abruptly to a dirt road and it was here that BMC drivers Fall and Aaltonen experienced suspension failures. Aaltonen made it to Kabul without loss of time by binding up the damaged suspension with his car's winch. The

last section into Teheran was on a road as good as the motorways in England.

As drivers Clark, Vaughan, Rutherford and Hopkirk noted, "Out of Tehran we were escorted by the local police chief. Once we'd cleared the suburbs he sped up to 100 mph and was having a ball. But Harry (Firth) got bored with that and pulled out and passed him and sped off at 125mph. We heard later that the police chief was really annoyed at that."

The road stretched off towards Kabul, some 1,480 miles away (time allowance 23 hours, 33 minutes) and was a good two-lane piece of blacktop. From Kandahar to Kabul, the road was dead straight for miles. Ian Vaughan commented, "We asked the locals why there was such a good road and they said, 'It was built by the Americans and Russians because they knew they were going to have a war here!'"

It was on this stretch of road that Harry Firth's car had an "incident." Co-driver Hoinville relates the story: "We had been cruising along at 120 mph or so when a rear tire burst. Harry quickly brought the car to a halt and Gary and I started to change it. It was night, pitch black, and there was not a soul around. Then out of nowhere appeared about six people who came up to

us talking in Afghani – we had to keep our eyes on our equipment because they'd steal it in a flash. Anyway, we got the wheel changed and blasted off into the night. It was an eerie experience."

Kabul was a compulsory rest stop for all crews. It was here that the English, European and Australian crews saw a different form of crowd control first-hand. The mounted police brutally knocked the spectators over with their horses to keep them out of the way. And as for their hotel accommodation Vaughan said, "The rooms were awful. In one corner was the shower-cum-toilet with cockroaches everywhere, the ceilings were 20 feet high and the shower hose was way up there. It was like standing under a waterfall."

Crossing the Khyber Pass at night was forbidden so the organizers arranged for the leading cars to be at the pass as dawn broke. Firth's Falcon GT was first on the road into Kabul although Clark was leading the marathon on points. The pass had a fearful reputation gained over many decades. What the crews found was that the road was no longer all dirt but had been bitumised and was in quite good condition. The Afghan authorities later apologized to the marathon organizers for the delay.

Left: Harry Firth powers through the notorious Khyber Pass in the early morning sun. Right: Firth's car being unloaded at Fremantle docks. Note the dents that so annoyed Harry.

THE CULTURAL EXPERIENCE

International relations are a delicate thing, as the crews discovered. Speaking on behalf of many of the teams, Graham Hoinville and teammate Gary Chapman related, "At the Pakistan-Indian border it was most amusing as well as being quite ridiculous. As you know there is a lot of tension between the two countries – anything the Pakistanis did, the Indians had to go one better. We were the first car at the checkpoint and after a very cordial welcome from the Pakistani border guards, we crossed to the Indian control point where a gorgeous Indian girl came up to us carrying a silver tray with a tea set of bone china and poured us each a cup of tea. With all good grace we declined."

On the road to Delhi there were hordes of people everywhere, all over the roads to the point that seeing where they were driving was difficult at times. In Delhi the crews again witnessed what we today would call police brutality. They beat the spectators with huge batons to get them out of the way of the marathon cars, and people collapsed, injured, into the roadside ditches and were left there.

South to Bombay (today Mumbai) – 858 miles in 22 hours, 51 minutes – where the teams had to dodge ox carts, sacred cows and trucks, again they were greeted enthusiastically by what seemed like the entire population of the city. The leading cars arrived ahead of schedule and had up to four days of rest and relaxation while they waited for the tail-end Charlies to reach Bombay.

The three Ford Falcon GTs were beginning to show the wisdom of the Australians' strategy when all they received were new disc pads and rear drum linings, a new set of dampers and little else. Team manager Gowland said, "People didn't believe us when we said that that was all we needed to do. Other teams, including our British and German friends, had to carry out major work on their remaining cars because they were driving them so hard. Credit must go to Harry and Ken Harper for the meticulous way in which they prepared all three cars."

Ian Vaughan added with a wry smile, "They really had to drive as hard as they did so they had plenty of time in the stops to rebuild their cars ready for the next stage!"

"I take my hat off to Des O'Dell," eventual winner Cowan said. "We never touched our car from London to Bombay; however, here we prepared it for the Australian section where we knew good quality fuel would be available. We took off the low-compression cylinder head and, putting a high-comp head on, replaced the rear axle-and-suspension assembly complete and the front struts. It was a brilliant strategy because it meant we had a virtually new car for the tough roads ahead of us."

Clark and Ove Andersson were presented with the Carrera Guards Trophy and a cheque for £2,000 for being the leader of the marathon at Bombay. Second at that stage were Simo Lampinen and Gilbert Staepalaere; Lucien Bianchi and Jean Ogier were third.

All the cars were impounded in the *parc fermé* where they were steam-cleaned before being loaded by sling onto the SS Chusan, destination Perth. The organizers had estimated that just 50 cars would get to Bombay; eventually 72 cars arrived to be loaded onto a ship that could take 70 cars at a pinch. The sailing took nine days to Fremantle, where the cars were unloaded.

On to Oz

Western Australian Premier David Brandt flagged the cars away from Gloucester Park at 4:00 in the afternoon on Saturday, Dec. 14, Clark being the first away followed by Firth. With the media build-up to the event in the preceding weeks, the crowd was huge. Because of the dusty conditions ahead, the organizers increased the time between cars from one minute to three, a wise move as it happened. Many had forecast that the marathon would be won or lost in Australia and so it proved to be. As Bill Tuckey said in his book *The History of Famous Australian Car Trials*, "Roger Clark beat his Cortina to death in Europe and lost the marathon in Australia; Zazada loitered through Europe and, with

Cowan, lost fewer points in the entire Australian section in a superlative drive, but left his run too late."

There had been rumors of police action along the Aussie route. Upon unloading, each car was impounded and given a roadworthy check – 27 cars failed it. And it happened again at Guildford, 10 miles out of Perth, where they had set up a roadblock to check and see if the teams had done their job. The rumblings from the international crews began to gather momentum.

From Perth the crews headed for the tiny gold mining town of Youanmi, 350 miles away with a time of seven hours allowed – an average speed of 50 mph – on hard-packed dirt.

From there they headed to Marvel Loch (243 miles in four hours, three minutes, an average of 60 mph) and encountered what could be described as the first difficult section in Australia. Vaughan: "The 'road'

Above: Roger Clark speeding through the Australian scenery. Below: Andrew Cowan lifts a wheel as he speeds towards victory.

Above: Winner Cowan was mobbed by the enthusiastic world media. Below: Winners Cowan, Malkin and Coyle being congratulated by New South Wales Premier Askin.

was little more than two wheel tracks across the flat countryside and each car threw up a huge dust cloud that hung in the air for ages and made life really difficult for those behind."

Lake King was a farther 119 miles away, this section being driven in the early hours of the morning. The cars were still on a one-lane track through the low scrub and dust was still a problem. Vaughan: "With all eight headlights blazing it was like driving through a tunnel because the undergrowth was right up to the edge of the track – I could lean on the brushwood to keep the car on the road!"

When the teams arrived in Lake King – a small town hundreds of miles from anywhere – they were greeted by several hundred enthusiastic spectators who had camped out on the edge of the town awaiting the marathon cars. It was here that Bruce Hodgson had an "incident."

"I was pushing pretty hard in the dust when I slid off a corner and clipped a tree that dented the side of

Above: Winner Cowan was mobbed by the enthusiastic world media. Below: Winners Cowan, Malkin and Coyle being congratulated by New South Wales Premier Askin.

the car. But what really annoyed me off was the guy driving the BMC service car who I swear was blocking me so the Austin 1800s of Hopkirk and Aaltonen could get farther in front of us. I gave him a couple of hefty nudges up the backside and eventually after many miles of this he let us through."

Clark was still leading the marathon, second-placed Ford Germany driver Lampinen in arrears by nine minutes.

Lake King to Ceduna was the longest single stretch in the marathon, 892 miles in 14 hours, 52 minutes. Some of it was on sealed roads – a temporary respite for the cars and crews – but the last 400 miles was over corrugated dirt roads. From Ceduna the crews raced on to Quorn via Port Augusta where the cars were serviced.

Clark was still leading at Ceduna but things had changed by the time cars started arriving at Port Augusta. Lucien Bianchi in a Citroën DS1 now led the marathon. Both the Fords of Lampinen (who was second into Port Augusta) and Clark were in urgent need of attention. Lampinen's Taunus had a complete new front suspension installed while Clark's car had limped into the service area with a very sick engine; it was running on three cylinders, having dropped a valve. In one of the many acts of chivalry in the marathon, teammates Ken Chambers and Eric Jackson offered Clark the cylinder head off their car in the hope that Clark could pull off a miraculous victory. With his Lotus-Cortina repaired, Clark drove the 26 miles from Port Augusta to Quorn in the dark in 16 minutes to be in third place.

THROUGH THE OUTBACK

The section from Quorn through to Mingary, only 347 miles in length and with a time of six hours, 57 minutes, took the cars through the picturesque Brachina Gorge, which was the first real test for both crews and cars in Australia. In typical Outback Australian style, the tracks were narrow, badly corrugated, pock-marked with craters big enough to destroy a car's suspension, and dipped unexpectedly down through steep-edged, rocky creek beds with numerous blind crests – in short, ideal rally country.

It was in the infamous Brachina Gorge section where McKay was balked by a Citroën that had collided with a kangaroo. Having passed it they came to a sandy section where George Reynolds lost control of the Monaro on a sweeping bend and rolled the car. They righted it and headed for Broken Hill, where doctors said Reynolds had a concussion and had lost a lot of blood. McKay headed straight for Sydney, taking no further part in the marathon.

At Mingary the order of cars was interesting as it was almost exactly half way through the Australian section; Bianchi in the Citroën DS21 was leading Clark in the Lotus-Cortina by four minutes, a further three minutes back was the Lampinen/Staepalaere Taunus 20M RS, then Aaltonen in the Austin 1800 Mark II and Cowan (something of a dark horse) in the Hillman Hunter.

All three Australian Ford Falcon GTs were in the top 10 at this stage, but as Ian Vaughan commented, "Although Bill Bourke and Keith Horner would have liked an outright victory, we had a conscious strategy at this stage of a team prize. We were definitely fast enough but we wanted to be there at the finish. Having said that, Zasada in the Porsche 911 S was gaining on me all the way across Australia. He was quick, especially on the flatter sections, but when it got rough I was able to pull away from him. If the marathon had gone another 20 miles I think he would have taken third place from me."

It was in the next stage, from Mingary south to Brookside in the Victorian Alps – 626 miles in 12 hours, 56 minutes – that more problems emerged with the police. Lampinen was cited for speeding and several other drivers were cautioned. Even though nothing came of it, the publicity it gathered did little good for the police.

Brookside to Omeo to Murrindal was a relatively short section, just 193 miles with one minute over four hours in which to do it. The problem was that it was through mountainous country and was driven at night. Vaughan was the best-placed Australian driver now while Clark's differential disintegrated in this section. He lost minimal time repairing it after he convinced a local Cortina owner, who had sat out to cheer the cars as they sped by, to give him the differential out of his car.

The cars turned north to Ingebyra, Numerella, Hindmarsh Station and Nowra in the southern highlands of New South Wales before descending down onto the plain and to Warwick Farm racecourse and the finishing line. Near Cooma the police really did a number on the marathon crews and came in for many derisory comments in the press when they announced that they were going to make an example of the "speed-crazed rally (sic) drivers." Paddy Hopkirk was quickest through the southern highlands, losing just one minute but Vaughan and Firth were there with him losing four and five minutes respectively. Sadly for Firth his Falcon GT's differential expired out of Hindmarsh Station but a signal to the service plane had the service

crew and a new diff on the ground almost immediately. He lost only 52 minutes making the repairs.

Despite the police presence, the driver of a Mini evaded a roadblock out of Nowra, about 100 miles from the finish, and crashed head-on into the leading car, Lucien Bianchi in the Citroën DS21, putting him out of the event virtually within sight of the finish line.

Paddy Hopkirk was the first driver to Warwick Farm and in a sporting gesture waited for the winning car, the Hillman Hunter of Andrew Cowan, to cross the line and he followed him over with Australian Ian Vaughan next.

Cowan was accorded a hero's welcome by the huge crowd who'd thronged to the venue to see the cars and crews. He acknowledged in his victory speech that Bianchi was the moral victor and that he felt sorry for him. Nevertheless, Cowan had displayed huge consistency during the entire event and as the old adage goes, to finish first, first you must finish. Cowan, Coyle and Malkin became celebrities when they returned to England, their victory taking them from respected competitors to international VIPs who would be feted throughout England and Europe for years to come.

Cowan today owns the Hillman Hunter he drove to victory, and Hopkirk's Austin 1800 Mk II is on display at the British Motor Industry Heritage Trust museum at Gaydon. Two out of the three Falcon GTs have been preserved, although interestingly enough none of the UK and German team cars seem to have survived for posterity.

Those who participated in the marathon agreed that it was the highlight of their careers. Speaking on behalf of his Ford teammates and echoing the sentiments of the Europeans, Vaughan had this to say: "Even though most of us had been involved in motorsport in some way for years, both before and after the marathon, that event was the first of its kind and that made it extra special for us all and it now occupies a special place in motoring folklore." AQ

THE STAKES

The crews were competing for The Daily Express Trophy.

The Stakes were:

1ST OUTRIGHT:

£10,000 plus The Daily Express Trophy and a free entry to the 1969 Safari Rally worth £60

2ND OUTRIGHT:

£3,000 plus the Daily Telegraph prize

3RD OUTRIGHT:

£2,000 plus a Daily Telegraph prize

SPECIAL AWARDS

£2,000
Best performance by an Australian crew; Daily Telegraph Prize

£2,000
First in general classification at Bombay plus Carreras/Guards Trophy

£500
Private entrants' award and Evening Standard Trophy

£50
Best performance by a vintage car, presented by Lord Montagu

£430
Ladies' first prize, by Cibie of England

THE PRIZE WINNERS

Prize	Car	No	Country	Driver	Points lost
1st	Hillman Hunter	75	England	Cowan	50
2nd	Austin 1800 Mark II	51	England	Hopkirk	56
3rd	Ford Falcon GT	24	Australia	Vaughan	62
4th	Porsche 911 S	58	Germany	Zasada	63
5th	Austin 1800 Mark II	61	England	Aaltonen	68
6th	Ford Falcon GT	29	Australia	Hodgson	70
7th	Ford Taunus 20M RS	92	Germany	Kleint	91
8th	Ford Falcon GT	2	Australia	Firth	114
9th	Citroën DS21	74	France	Neyret	123
10th	Ford Lotus-Cortina	48	England	Clark	144

PRIVATEERS

Prize given by the London Evening Standard

1	Porsche 911	55	Germany	Herrmann 1	95
2	Mercedes-Benz 280	32	England	Barker	264
3	Saab 96 Estate	56	England	Percy	438
4	Mercedes-Benz 200D	62	Australia	Praznovszky	455
5	Peugeot 404	83	Eire	Cotton	470

TEAM PRIZE

Prize given by Ladbroke's of London

1st	Ford Falcon GT	Australia	246 points
2nd	BMC 1800 Mark II	England	554 points
3rd	BMC 1800 Mark II	England	1414 points
4th	Moskvitch 408	Russia	1987 points

LADIES

Prize given by Cibie of England

1	Volvo 145	33	England	Miss E Gadd	2399 pts
2	Ford Lotus-Cortina	93	Eire	Miss R Smith	6139 pts
3	Morris 1100	41	Australia	Miss E Westley	8111 pts

BEST AUSTRALIAN CREWS

1	Ford Falcon GT	24	Vaughan	62 pts
2	Ford Falcon GT	29	Hodgson	70
3	Ford Falcon GT	2	Firth	114
4	Volvo 144 S	12	Tubman	146
5	Holden Monaro GTS	76	Ferguson	69
6	Volvo 144 S	43	Welinski	171
7	Holden Monaro GTS	68	Whiteford	173
8	Austin 1800 Mark II	31	Green	332
9	Mercedes-Benz 200D	62	Praznovszky	455
10	Morris 1100	41	Westley	8111

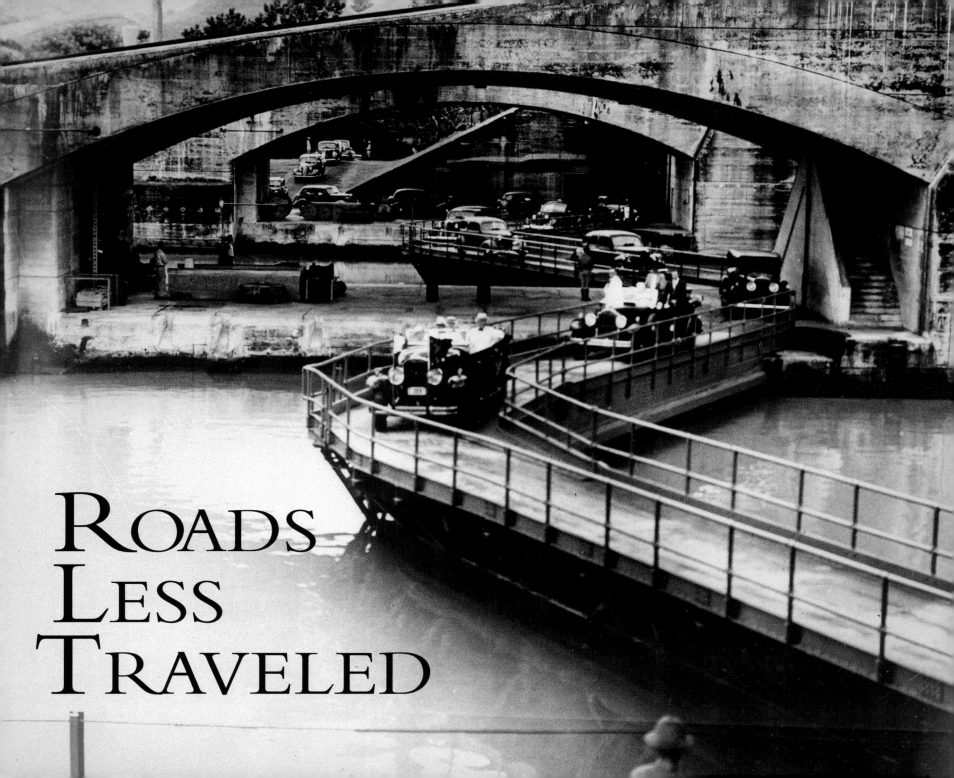

ROADS
LESS
TRAVELED

PREWAR MOTORING IN THE PANAMA CANAL ZONE

T he Panama Canal is one of mankind's greatest achievements and is a key conduit for international shipping. Each year more than 14,000 ships pass through the canal, carrying more than 205 million tons of cargo. The primary achievement in Panama was in building the infrastructure necessary to complete the canal, a project that depended on automobiles in private and government hands. Here, we explore motoring on the Isthmus of Panama when the canal was still young.

Opposite: The automobiles carrying President Roosevelt's party made a neat serpentine pattern as they crossed the driveway made from closing the mitered tops of the lock gates at Pedro Miguel. Above: A 1917 street scene in the Panama Canal Zone at Gatun.

BY BROOKS T. BRIERLEY

Within the grand scope of building the Panama Canal were innovations supporting other transportation systems such as the automobile. They were fostered by the new towns built in the Canal Zone – such as Balboa on the Pacific Coast (the administrative capital of the Zone), Cristobal on the Atlantic, and Gatun inland – incorporating the beginnings of a model road system of paved streets with curbs and sidewalks. The automobile was officially recognized there on Dec. 3, 1910, when the first automobile license was issued. Additional vehicles came slowly; by the end of December 1910 there were a total of six cars licensed. By September 1912 that total had risen to 65 automobiles.

The canal's official opening was to be a grand parade of ships, including historic vessels such as Admiral Dewey's flagship, the USS *Olympia*. But the preface to World War I ruined these plans; the canal simply began its day-to-day business without fanfare. Barge traffic began quietly in May 1914, with sugar cargo from Hawaii. On Aug. 14, 1914, a U.S. War Department passenger/cargo steamship, the *Ancon*, arrived from New York to officially open and traverse the canal. Col. George Goethals, the builder of the canal and subsequently the governor of the Zone, was on board, together with President Porras of Panama. Newspaper reports added that the *Ancon* was fully loaded – this was a working voyage, too.

Automotive housekeeping chores were well underway then, as well. There does not appear to be much delegation of authority in the Zone at the time, even the purchase of a Ford Model T had to be approved by the governor of the Canal Zone. The breadth of the process could be interesting. For example, in 1914, the Health Department needed to purchase a car, the choice narrowing to a Buick costing $925 and a Ford priced at $585. Both cars had acceptable service and parts available in Panama. The health officer, who was to use the car, preferred the Buick. But few knew much about evaluating cars, including the chief quartermaster, who oversaw purchases. The Panama Canal motor car inspector stationed at Culebra, Samuel Grier Jr., became involved and wrote a short but persuasive

The ferryboat *President Roosevelt* entering West Slip June 12, 1934.

opinion – he always capitalized the word "car" in his memos – emphasizing Ford's price difference and operating advantages. Raising an issue rarely pertinent today, Grier's memo to the governor also emphasized that the simplicity of the Ford Model T allowed it to be driven by the employee, not requiring the expense of a chauffeur.

At this time there were no meaningful roads outside the Canal Zone, only trails. A National Highway was developed with some feeder roads within the country of Panama in the 1920s. At the beginning of the Depression about 900 miles of roadway existed, much of it very crude and virtually unusable during the rainy

season. It was not a place for touring. The developed countryside of Panama was primarily agricultural, and included both large American-owned plantations and local farms. There, a little bus called "chiva," made from a used-car chassis, was given a locally crafted utility body. It was the primary means of carrying the local inhabitants and their produce to market. In sharp contrast, the 200 miles of roads in the city and the Zone were paved and considered passable in all weather. Even so, the Canal Zone's business and government purposes were overwhelming – it was not a resort – requiring nearly all cars to be basic open models and sedans. A few limousines were there, but the way of life did not justify the use of formal town cars or special coachbuilt automobiles.

Once removed from canal operation areas and residential compounds, the Zone's road system resembled a series of narrow country lanes. There was no bridge across the canal. A ferryboat service called Thatcher Ferry transported both cars and people from the east to west sides of the canal. The tops of the gates of the locks at Pedro Miguel, when closed, were built to include a single-lane road to bridge the canal, but only for special use.

The Canal Zone's interrelationship with the Republic of Panama led to adopting Panamanian traffic rules, which included driving on the left side of the road. Geographic limitations – the Canal Zone extended only five miles from each side of the canal – were said to be too difficult to build a road to go from the Pacific to the Atlantic within the Zone. Feasibility discussions may have involved competitive issues: the American government-owned Panama Railroad, a large operation, had a monopoly on land transportation traversing the Zone. That made the best roads local routes, such as the Colon Gatun Road, going from Cristobal and the adjacent Panamanian city of Colon inland to the Gatun locks. Later, in the mid-1930s, the military advantage of a road crossing the Isthmus, called the Trans-Isthmian Highway, became increasingly important. The American government conducted lengthy negotiations with Panama to modify the Treaty of 1903, which created the Zone, to build it.

THE PANAMANIAN MARKET

In the 1920s, when a new shipment of automobiles arrived at a colonial location, it was the catalyst for a great promotion. Panama was no exception. When 18 new Buicks arrived on the SS *Cristobal* (part of regular steamship service from the American East Coast) in March 1923, the dealer, Panazone Garage, took a full-page ad in the local *Star and Herald* newspaper. "Eighteen Buick Cars Received in One Shipment," it extolled, with an illustration of each

A Model T Ford on top of one of the Pedro Miguel Lock guard gates. There was provision for railings on the interior side of the gate, but they are not installed here.

model. All were open models: 10 seven-passenger touring cars, five five-passenger touring cars, one four-passenger sport model and two five-passenger four-cylinder cars.

Capriles Y Co. Ltd., located on H Street at the corner of 17th in Panama City, was like most distributors in Panama, selling both car (Hupmobile) and truck (Fageol) lines. Fageol "compound trucks" had the distinction of being the first West Coast-made motor vehicle to arrive in Panama, in September 1927. They arrived in Balboa and were driven from the Canal Zone to the Panama City showroom. By the standards of the times, the Fageols enjoyed modest sales – in December, five trucks of the shipment had been sold.

Panama and the Canal Zone was a very competitive automobile market. The commercial attaché in the Department of Commerce office in Panama City kept close watch of the sales representatives. In February 1928 he reported to headquarters in Washington that 32 makes of cars were represented by 16 agencies in Panama. The Auburn, Chandler, Cleveland and Jordan dealers in the Canal Zone were known for selling at cost to get into the market. That made a very difficult situation for someone representing a smaller, less-capitalized manufacturer. When Elcar, Moon and Gardner sought help from the U.S. Department of Commerce to enter the market, the companies' market research and due diligence included blunt discussions about this unusual competitiveness.

Newspapers were the primary source of automotive

news. The *Star and Herald*, the oldest in the Zone, ran a special automotive section in the Sunday edition. Most of it was press release-type news from sources in the United States. Some presentations were very special. In 1925, Kelly-Springfield tires had racecar driver Ralph de Palma write a series of 10 short stories, called lessons, on "The Art of Driving." They included subjects such as "Instructions for Chauffeurs." Kelly-Springfield's Panama representative, Panazone Garage, sponsored these stories.

One of the *Star and Herald*'s competitors, the *Panama American*, a morning newspaper, did not have any automotive stories, but Sunday's edition included a big "Automobile Directory" column, with car, truck and accessory names, dealer locations and phone numbers. About half the makes of cars being sold were represented there. Some of the January 1929 entries included interesting bits of information: Chandler had two dealers, E. M. Reinhold in Cristobal and G. Edgar Murphy in Balboa, with the same Cristobal 1596 telephone number. Generally, the more popular marques, such as Buick, Chevrolet and Chrysler, had representation on both sides of the Isthmus of Panama, but not the lesser-known marques. Harry Nicholls represented Dodge in Panama City then; Mac's Tourist Service, tucked away between 2nd and 3rd streets, one block west of G Street, in Colon, was the Marmon agent. Paige's dealer Frederick's Auto & Supply Service, at 16th and Broadway in Colon, revealed its time in business with its Colon 6 telephone number. Frederick's also handled Oldsmobile, using the Colon 5 telephone for that part of the business. Lam Bros., the Hudson Essex dealer in Colon, gave the telephone number Colon 99.

The Zone's mix of business and government tasks easily included many Ford Model Ts, but as the Zone's mission and its infrastructure were enlarged and refined, a much greater variety of cars and body styles was used. The change came about in the mid-1920s. As late as 1923, the privately held automotive population in Panama and the Canal Zone was mostly Fords (600) and Buicks (375). There were 130 Ford trucks and buses; the next most popular was Dodge

Cars waiting to drive onto Thatcher Ferry at East Slip, June 12, 1934.

with nine. At the Panama Canal itself, the cars that were used included 52 Fords, five Dodges and one Cadillac. Remembering that trucks at the time were often modified cars, the truck population included 153 Ford trucks, 21 Kelly-Springfields and five Dodges. It is not clear how the single Velie truck was used.

During the Depression, there was an incentive for employees of the canal and its affiliated Panama Railroad Company to own automobiles by allowing

duty-free import of automobiles. That was also one of the sources of friction between the Canal Zone and the native Panamanians. By 1932, a survey of licensed cars in the Zone listed 6,303 private cars, 624 taxis (then called "hacking") and 1,082 official vehicles (a mix of passenger cars and commercial vehicles). It was a dramatic change from six years earlier – 1926 – in both number and variety of cars. Ford was most popular then, of course. Chevrolet was a strong second

The USS *Iowa* leaving Pedro Miguel Lock to enter Miraflores Lake in Feb. 10, 1923.

in 1932, but it was Studebaker that occupied second place in 1926. Among the more obscure makes represented were two De Vaux and an Armstrong-Siddeley. Buick was the most popular make of taxi, yet the number of different automotive brands surely encouraged car enthusiasts to seek out the lone Kissel or Marmon for a unique treat, too. Both Packards and Fiats were licensed under private and official vehicles. Even so, it was a late-1920s Cadillac touring car that carried President Roosevelt on his 1938 visit to the Canal, which included driving across the single-lane road created from the top of one of the lock gates.

Within these statistics are everyday automotive issues of the time that, from today's perspective, can appear to be somewhat glossy anecdotes. One was the juggling of official car assignments: In 1934, two Cadillacs assigned to J. L. Schley, who was both the governor of the Panama Canal and the president of the Panama Railroad Company, were returned to the Motor Transportation Division pool of cars. The chauffeur assigned to these cars was transferred from the Panama Railroad to the Panama Canal employee rolls.

A number of vehicles in the Zone were used as buses. In October 1933, the Port Captain of the Marine Division in Balboa, on the Pacific side of the Zone, was leasing three mini buses – a 1930 Ford station wagon and two six-passenger 1926 Dodges described as "side seaters" – from the Transportation Division of the Panama Canal Company. The Dodges were reaching the end of their useful lives, with odometer readings of 189,806 and 210,113 miles, respectively. The process to replace them began with a specific proposal written by the Port Captain, in memorandum form, to purchase two Chevrolet one-ton chassis. Interestingly, bodies were to be built in the Zone's own Transportation shops. The proposal included some Depression-era price comparisons; the 1926 Dodges had cost $1,298.68 each, whereas prices of a new Chevrolet was estimated to be $700. Also within the memo was a calculation that the lease payments for the Dodges had been about eight times original cost; not surprisingly, the Chevrolets were purchased outright.

Dodge had been very aggressive in seeking Canal Zone business. As early as December 1921, representative Harry Nicholls, who took care to have both Panama and Canal Zone addresses printed on colorful head-office-style company stationary, wrote directly to Colonel Morris, then governor of the canal. The Motor Transportation Department was contemplating leasing all its vehicles when Nichols asked to submit a proposal. The two Dodges being replaced in 1933 had been part of those early automotive transactions.

There appear to have been continual exceptions to parking official vehicles in protected garages and a space called "the corral." Employees were required to verify the exception in great detail. Being on call 24 hours a day for emergencies seems to have been a common part of many assignments. Two official cars assigned to a coaling plant, where there were "practically no coaling operations," were the catalyst for a vehicle inquiry. Another problem was to ensure that a car parked at night without a garage was properly protected. Sometimes, a canvas tarp placed over the vehicle at night during the rainy season was enough. Sometimes there was a change in parking place. These matters continued to be handled in a formal manner by senior management. The superintendent of the Panama

Left: This 3 1/2-ton Pierce-Arrow truck, USN #5729, was assigned to the Canal Zone's Fleet Air Force Base, the Coco Solo Naval Air Station, when this photo was taken on April 4, 1934. Right: A 1920s view of I Street in Panama City.

Railroad Company was one of the officials who wrote letters to department heads, who in turn wrote to their supervisors, for explanations of the variances.

One of the most intriguing stories involves a car in the 1932 Canal Zone registrations. It is outlined in a letter dated April 18, 1933, by R.W. Ryden, a superintendent for the Department of Operation and Maintenance to the Chief of Police and Fire Division in Balboa Heights. The letter began: "There is an old automobile within the Balboa Shops premises which the owner has apparently abandoned; for the machine has not been moved in several months. The automobile is a Locomobile bearing a 1932 Canal Zone license plate. The number of this plate is 4584." The car's fate

was sealed when it took the most convenient transient parking spot, located next to a well-used storehouse. Surviving correspondence indicates it was removed the following day.

Panama and Canal Zone regulations required their own licenses to run in their respective areas. The close interaction of the two areas led nearly all Zone cars to carry Panamanian license plates.

At year end 1934, there were also 1,199 official government cars, buses and trucks assigned to the different parts of the canal business. The Zone was home to the Fifteenth Naval District, a relatively modest-size entity centered on the Coco Solo submarine base and

air station, plus facilities in Balboa. It was said to be an unusual district for being without significant naval vessels. The commandant was an admiral, assigned all the trappings of his office, including an imposing home and a limousine. Despite the limousine's limited use – primarily to take the admiral from his home to the office – the commuting must have added a bit of pageantry to the isthmus' working routine.

Ford Motor Co. provided the Canal Zone with special automotive status when the company established an assembly plant in Cristobal in the late 1920s to service distribution through Central America and Chile. The plant was supplied directly from Ford's Kearny, N.J., factory. The idea was to bring the vehicles closer

Left: Looking south at Paraiso Cutoff in 1931 shows a completed stretch of the new concrete Gaillard Highway being built across the Isthmus. A close look at the Ford Model A roadster in the corner of the photo reveals it is a working roadster – a big trunk has replaced the rumbleseat. Right: Crossing Juan Diaz Bridge in the Republic of Panama in March 1917.

to their sales point, reducing the lead times for dealer orders. Nearly 1,700 cars and trucks were processed this way in 1928, about 500 in the first two months of 1929. Reports stated the vast majority of these were re-exported to Colombia.

The Panazone Garage Co. was also reported to have a considerable re-export business in the late 1920s. Volume for 1928 was said to be about 900 cars and trucks.

As the American automobile industry changed in the late 1920s, driven by the consolidation of manufacturing and new technologies, dealers in the isthmus changed their sales and services accordingly. When Duco paint replaced high-maintenance varnish finishes, there was a great improvement in the maintenance of bodies. Walker and Hopkins,

the Studebaker agent located on Central Avenue in Panama City, set up a new plant to refinish cars with the new process. Another favorite promotion was used by Chrysler-Plymouth dealer Day and Night Garage, which paraded new cars through downtown Panama City, past competitor showrooms.

Business changes took place in Panama just as in the States: Panazone Garage Co. sold Buicks in the 1920s from showrooms in Panama City and Colon. It was a good business. Not only were Buicks popular as passenger cars, they were by far the most important taxi used in the Zone. By 1930, Frederick's Garage had succeeded Panazone in Colon. Nash was aggressively represented in Panama City by the Nash Motor Garage, which also handled Royal Cord tires, Tidewater Oil products and AC spark plugs. They opened a new

showroom at the corner of West 17th and H streets in March 1930. *Star and Herald* readers could see Nash Motor ads in Sunday's automobile section, easily distinguished from competitors' smaller ads.

THE DEPRESSION

The Depression did not significantly affect canal business. A 1935 U.S. Department of Commerce study revealed that Panama automobiles were not being parked for lack of need or shortage of maintenance funds, as was the case in other countries. Evidence of this was in the 75 to 100 vehicles estimated to be temporarily out of service, the result of normal maintenance issues.

Above: This scene of a Chrysler parked by the dentist's office at Gatun on Nov. 5, 1935, offers an example of Canal Zone genre. Right: President Roosevelt's August 1938 visit to the Canal Zone was the catalyst for some ceremonies at Pedro Miguel, which the President watched from an older Cadillac touring car.

The Panama Canal was indeed a unique locale during the Depression era. Somehow, the Canal Zone's status magnified the arrival of important people, likely helped by the area's compact size. When Charles Lindbergh flew to the Zone in January 1928, scouting the practicality of establishing airline routes from the United States to South America, Panama issued two special stamps commemorating the visit. A special post office cancellation was made for the day of his arrival to give the stamps even greater value.

President Franklin D. Roosevelt visited the Canal Zone several times before World War II, always arriving on the cruiser USS *Houston* (Roosevelt was reported to work on his stamp collection there). He would leave the ship and proceed by automobile to

ceremonies at one of the naval installations, rejoining the ship as it went through the canal. Every detail of Roosevelt's itinerary was reported. In October 1935, President Arias of Panama met Roosevelt at the *Houston*'s dock. Roosevelt wore a Panama hat for the occasion. They rode in President Arias' touring car to Fort Clayton for a troop review. There was a luncheon served at the officers club; a highball was tucked into the list of entries on the printed presidential menu, which included turkey, steamed carrots and biscuits.

Roosevelt's Aug. 6, 1938, visit also began with the arrival of the *Houston* in Balboa. Governor Ridley and new Panamanian President Arosemena both were there to meet him. President Arosemena was known for his fast driving (Roosevelt liked a modest pace).

The day included a salute and review of the troops at Fort Clayton, with Roosevelt seated in one of the Zone's old Cadillac touring cars. There were also a series of stops at different locales, such as inspecting a newly constructed ammunition dump and inspecting a new five-mile-long concrete section of the Pan American highway. With the coming of World War II widely anticipated, much of the president's time was spent inspecting improvements to the military installations, such as new planes. Road construction, both for a cross-isthmus highway and supporting roads within Panama, was a major topic of discussion. It is a comment on the times that canal traffic was not stopped during Roosevelt's visit. He had the opportunity to see full operations, including greetings to

Left: A May 1922 view of the Panama Railroad Company station in Panama City. Above: A touring car stopped back of Old Corozal, on the Panama Road in the Panamanian countryside in 1917.

the SS *Rangitane*, on the way from New Zealand to London, as it passed through the Miraflores Locks. The president's Cadillac led a motor procession across the narrow zigzag driveway, set on top of the Pedro Miguel lower lock gates, to the other side of the canal. Photographs of that part of the ride indicate it was a breathtaking experience.

The Depression fostered a closer look at the quality of life in the Canal Zone. In 1932 there were Panamanian protests against the free import of cars for employees of the canal and the railroad companies. Even so, the idyllic views of the Zone expressed in

the 1920s remained relatively unchanged. Civilian pay was higher than for equivalent positions in the United States, and included 60 days of paid leave each year. Then, military budget cutting led to housing shortages for personnel and their families. A number of those assigned to the submarine base were forced to live outside the Canal Zone. The strictness of the Zone's rules, which included Prohibition, quickly clashed with the more casual local lifestyle. In late 1936, the grit in these issues became public knowledge from an unusual source in a story called "Canal Expose" published in the venerable *Literary Digest*. Revelations of

a vibrant nightlife and tenement-quality housing next door to the Zone peaked when it was found that these indiscretions took place on land owned by the Panama Railroad Company, an entity whose stock was entirely owned by the United States government.

Yet, the Canal Zone's popular image of vessels making their way effortlessly through the isthmus never wavered. While most were various-size warships and freighters, glamorous vessels were seen in the locks, such as the Canadian Pacific flagship *Empress of Britain* and the great German Blue Ribband liner *Bremen*. Scenes like these and J.P. Morgan's legendary yacht *Corsair* passing through Gaillard Cut – images capable of inspiring fine paintings – made certain the canal's mystique remained untouched.

Cars & Castles
in Spain

THE CAN COSTA FOUNDATION

*I*t is not a simple task to catch Joaquín Folch-Rusiñol Corachán in non-racing attire, when he's not getting in or out of a Formula 1 car. On this rare occasion when he appeared without his lucky helmet, the Spanish collector opened his Can Costa Foundation gate to be introduced exclusively to AQ's readers.

Folch at the starting line in Nürburgring, at the wheel of the ex-Fittipaldi McLaren M23.

BY MARIO LAGUNA

In his long career as a devoted automobilist, Joaquín Folch-Rusiñol Corachán, 55, has driven everything on wheels – front-, rear- and mid-engined cars, seriously and successfully. He is familiar with drum and disc brakes, whether on GTs, lightweight racers or prototypes. Consecutively, in 1993 and 1994 at the wheel of his Lotus 23B, he won the European Championship for historic race cars. Today, he focuses on the Grand Prix Masters and the FIA Formula 1 Historic Championship. In these disciplines he has proved a brilliant contender by his five victories, two second and two third places for the nine historic Formula 1 races in which he saw action in 2007.

Working as president of a company with a staff of 1,000 people and racing a ground-effect 1980 Brabham-Ford BT49C at Spa-Francorchamps should share a few similar emotions. You make the wrong decision and you are out of competition. Both activities need quick thinking and good reflexes. In 1989, young Folch took the helm of Industrias Titán, founded in 1917, a 120,000-square-meter chemical factory, which produces and distributes paints, enamels and varnishes in 500 different forms. Folch is also a member of the board of Banco de Sabadell, a Spanish commercial bank with branches in the United States, France and Great Britain.

Preservation of automotive history is a less stressful exercise. The challenges are different, although not less demanding in terms of dedication. For this purpose, the first requirement is a home of convenient proportions. Folch spotted an ideal place to park his growing automotive collection at a family property just a stone's throw from Barcelona, and from there he created the Can Costa Foundation. If one could describe only with words what shelters the thick walls of the restored 17th-century house, many would remain incredulous, like reading a Castles in Spain fable. In 1955, Joaquín Folch, grandfather of our host, bought a 45-hectare farm for cattle. On the approximate 110-acre property, he also grew fruit trees and vineyards. The old farmers' building was refurbished and used as the family summer house. Childhood memories of wide-open playgrounds are now told alongside

Above: A Ferrari 312T5 (front) and 312T3 welcome you to the alleys of the Can Costa Foundation. Below: The impressive 1960 Lancia Flaminia Zagato with double bubble roof.

Left: A 1954 Pegaso Z-102 Touring in front of the restored Can Costa 17th-century farm. Above: The Aston Martin DB4GT is a wolf in Superleggera skin.

Folch's big toys displayed over the 3,000 square meters that the Mediterranean garage occupies.

A modern, busy city in northeastern Spain, Barcelona was the world capital for athletic sports during the 1992 Olympic Games, the same year the foundation was born. Barcelona has a rich motoring tradition. Since the early '20s, racing events took place in the nearby Sitges circuit. The 1923 banking, kidney-shaped circuit was one of the first purpose-built race tracks in Europe, following England's pioneer Brooklands (1907) and Monza (1922). After the war,

the Spanish Grand Prix brought much excitement to the urban Pedralbes circuit in 1946. Also in the streets of Barcelona, the legendary Montjuich circuit witnessed many epic Formula 1 battles. The tragic closing of Montjuich in 1975 made way to the modern Montmeló complex, which is in use today. Respectively, prewar and postwar Hispano-Suiza and Pegaso factories were located in Barcelona, followed by Fiat-licensed and then Volkswagen-owned Seat.

In this rich automotive environment, young Folch went with his father to Montjuich races, where the spark for motoring passion was triggered, as it was for many of his school companions. The difference is that Folch waited patiently through years of university and business responsibilities to realize his dream of sitting in the very cars he once saw speeding by at the races.

FROM ALFA TO ZAGATO

Inside the old Can Costa house, ancient pieces of religious art mix with the colors of motorbikes, cars and hunted treasures of automobilia. Carefully chosen models take a special place in customized glass cases, but rather than collect indiscriminate hundreds, on display are a selected few, some commissioned from renowned professionals, such as the McLaren M23.

Folch's strategy for preserving cars involves flexibility when acquiring targets. Originality is a must for a piece of motor history, while modifications are welcome in battle horses for fighting rivals in long-distance commemorative events, including the Carrera Panamericana or the Mille Miglia. When restoring his Pegaso Z-102 with Touring berlinetta coachwork,

dynamic design most sports cars would follow. The Cisitalia 202 coupe in the Can Costa collection is a late-1950s survivor, similar to the one Italian director Michelangelo Antonioni had chosen

boasting loads of performance and refinement.

In the hands of Folch, the Flaminia has been preserved from the commonly known weakness of Zagato bodies, its scant protection against rust. Zagato bodies of the 1960s were built to save weight and go racing,

Folch takes his model collection very seriously, even the childrens' versions. Here we see Bugatti and Maserati examples, among others.

Folch had in mind several improvements that would allow the alloy quad-cam V8 to compete in future pre-1957 revivals. The car, no. 0156, was used in the 1950s by noted Spanish driver Alex Soler-Roig in local rallies. In isolated postwar Spain, the Pegaso was intended as a foreign currency hunter, a mission that it failed – from a total production of nearly 100, most found domestic homes.

Unlike the more gracious Pegasos by Touring, the earlier ENASA (Empresa Nacional de Autocamiones, Sociedad Anónima) bodies were designed in-house and built from scratch. Although the true unconditional Pegaso fan will always fiercely support the 100-percent Spanish car that is a Z-102 in ENASA berlinetta form, the expensive, imported Touring Superleggera bodies bring balance, lightness, purity and harmony to the flying horse. Even having in mind that a berlinetta ENASA won its class at Pebble Beach in 1994, indulge the author to be on the majority's side of those who rather would take home a Touring variation.

Little is left to say about Cisitalia after you read AQ Vol. 32 No. 3, where Jonathan Stein wrote about the coupe by Battista Farina that set the pattern for aero-

for debutant eMiss Italia Lucia Bose, who starred in *Cronaca di un amore* (1950). Bose's car was a more delicate spider, however; the low body oozes an exquisite functional elegance.

You understand Antonioni really loved fine cars when you find another exotic in his film *La notte* (1961), where a Lancia Flaminia Zagato is the brief iron escort for Jeanne Moreau. Can Costa's elegant Flaminia brings memories of the influential film, despite its appearance under a sunny sky instead of riding the wet streets of Milan. The Flaminia is a genuine classic, one of the ultimate machines to cruise in sober GT fashion,

not to last, which is why they are so exotic now. A well-preserved Zagato is rarer than old porcelains and deserves all the indoor care the owner is able to provide. As with Formula 1 cars, their beauty is circumstantial.

Although an Aston Martin DB4, dressed in the finest Superleggera skin, is enough to satisfy the most fastidious collector, many true nut-and-bolt lovers of traditional British machines go for the subtle differences found in her GT sister, introduced at the 1959 London Motor Show. One of the differences not defined as subtle is the higher price for one of the 74 units the factory built to 302 bhp. In February 2008, during the

Rétromobile car show in Paris, a twin-plug cylinder-head 1962 DB4 GT, which failed to sell, was put into auction for an estimated value of $1.5 million.

Viewed from the front, the GT is distinguishable by its headlamps with Plexiglas covers, a standard feature for the later DB5. Incidentally, the distinctive DB4 Aston grille appears again in the reshaped DB5 and DB6 brands, two models also in the collection. A mere thousand DB5s were built, with all-alloy quad-cam 3.995cc six-cylinder engine, capable of 282 bhp transmitted to the tarmac through a ZF five-speed manual gearbox.

Deciding to build a special Aston Martin section in his garage was not difficult. Some of the aforementioned were already in the family when Folch started collecting cars. Since the early 1960s, Alberto Folch, Joaquín's father, imported Aston Martins, an activity shared with similar jobs for Lotus and Jensen. Some of the Aston Martins the Folchs used daily as personal and family transportation are now carefully maintained and looked after by the foundation. A more recent Vanquish acquisition is also nested in the collection.

Another recognizable marque at Can Costa is Alfa Romeo, one of the most consolidated among other century-old automotive legends. The 1900 Touring was a design by Federico Formenti, who made a clean body, looking like a spider with a hard top. It is a very well-balanced car with front and rear volumes in perfect harmony. In 1937, Touring introduced its Superleggera system, which uses a tubular steel frame covered by aluminum sheets. The clever solution for light and rigid bodies was inspired from the older aircraft Weymann method, with wooden frames and synthetic leather instead.

The car loses its charming balance to become more aggressive in Zagato form. Distinctive bonnet fresh-air intakes and lowered front end make the cars recognizable on spot. Some Zagatos have the peculiar double bubble roof, which allows more clearance above the heads when the driver and his companion are wearing helmets. The Zagato in the foundation was raced by famous Escudería Montjuich, which saw action in local rallies with Juan Figueras behind the wheel.

Choosing a standout among the wealth of such gems is difficult, but perhaps the shining star at Can Costa is a Grand Prix Maserati 250 F, raced in 1956 by Francisco Godia, who finished fourth in both the German and Italian Grands Prix. Juan Manuel Fangio used a similar car in 1954, which helped him win the Drivers World Championship. Until the present time, with Fernando Alonso at the top of the F1 World Championship in 2005 and 2006, Godia was the highest Spanish entry placed in Grand Prix races.

When discussion shifts to GT Ferraris – a pair of 275GTBs are in the collection – Folch focuses instead on his preferred subject, the more restricted world of F1 cars and the performance they deliver in its purest expression. In an F1 Ferrari, nothing interferes between organic and inorganic parts, as the driver becomes the soul of sophisticated metal, high-tech rubber and composite melting. A Formula 1 car begs to go to the track often, if even for its survival. No need to remind this to Folch, whose more enjoyable "season" miles are consumed in the finest circuits on the Continent and in Great Britain. Folch can be found racing at Spa-Francorchamps and Nürburgring.

The GP history of both Can Costa F1 Ferraris, 312T-3/32 and 312T-5/42, is short. In 1978, T-3 was Jacques Villeneuve's car at Kyalami and was raced by Carlos Reutemann in Monaco and Germany. T-5 had its best results in 1980 when it was factory-entered for Villeneuve, again at Kyalami, and for Jody Scheckter in Argentina and Brazil. The flat-12, 3-liter engine was

A splendid Alfa Romeo 1900 Zagato (left), with its more sober companion Alfa Romeo 1900 Touring (right). Both are of 1955 vintage.

designed by Mauro Forghieri. Identifying the model, T stands for transversale or transverse gearbox, meant to reduce the suspended weight behind the rear axle, centering as much weight as possible between front and rear axels. The 312s were going to be the last 12-cylinder Ferraris, before the arrival of the little 1500cc V6 turbo engines in the summer of 1980 for the new 126C model.

Unlike the Ferraris, the Lotus 91, designed by Colin Chapman for the 1982 season, was used extensively all year long by Elio de Angelis. Car 91/8 claimed a thrilling championship victory in the Austrian Grand Prix, raced at the fast Zeltweg circuit.

For winning at Nürburgring, Folch's favorite tool is a 1974 McLaren-Ford M23, a car counting eight victo-ries in period F1 races. It was the first F1 car designed by Gordon Coppuck and the actual car driven to victory by Jochen Mass in the last Formula 1 G.P. raced at Montjuich in spring 1975.

The author was 23 when he went with friends to the Barcelona magical mountain on April 27 for another exciting race and saw M23/8 for the first time. There was controversy in the air with pilots complaining and demonstrating against poor safety conditions. Emerson Fittipaldi refused to take the start and was in a plane returning home when Stommelen crashed at the end of the pits lane and the flying parts of his Embassy-Hill killed four. Twelve more were injured. The author was 200 meters ahead of the crash. At the wheel of M23/8, Mass was leading the race when it

Left: An exceptional example of integrated aerodynamic design, this 1959 Cisitalia 202 coupe is advanced for its age. Note the split windshield. Above: Significant for Spanish motoring history, this 1957 Maserati 250F was piloted by Francisco Godia.

was abruptly stopped, so he won. Previously, Fittipaldi had won in Canada on September 1974 with the same car. In 1976, the car was committed to James Hunt, winning six G.P. races in Spain, France, Germany, the Netherlands, Canada and the United Estates (east).

For Spa-Francorchamps, Folch prefers a Brabham-Ford BT49C he borrows from Formula 1 boss Bernie Ecclestone. Designed by Gordon Murray, the ground-effect Brabham BT49C/10 was built in 1980 for the United States G.P., where it was kept as a spare car. Then, no. 10 was updated in 1981 and driven by Nelson Piquet at Kyalami. After previous seasons using V12 Alfa Romeo engines, Brabham returned BT49C to V8 Cosworth power. In spite of its lack of significant G.P. history, the Brabham is terribly fast in the hands of Folch, who calls the Swiss Kumschick Racing team for technical assistance. The 2993cc Ford-Cosworth

Above: Motorcycles are found in more and more personal and public collections, and Can Costa is no exception. Folch's guests can admire 250 models, inclcuding Montesa, Bultaco, Derbi, Ducati, Yamaha, Honda, Harley-Davidson, Norton and Triumph. Below: Folch discusses the 2007 Nürburgring race with Fredy Kumschick, his team manager.

DFV V8 engine delivers 470 bhp at 11,100 rpm to carry a weight of 580 kg, driver excluded.

Occasionally, some cars leave the foundation to go to events around Europe. That was recently the case for a Ford GT40, serial no. 1019, which Folch brought to celebrate the 75th Anniversary of Montjuich in October 2007, before the car was sent to England. Folch is fond of a car that was conceived to be the Le Mans Ferrari killer in 1966. Escudería Montjuich sponsored the team Godia/Muir for the 1968 Barcelona six-hour race. They won the race with GT40/1019, one of Folch's favorite cars, perhaps because he witnessed the race when he was 15.

Although we cannot look at it in detail, special attention should be paid to the impressive motorbike collection, hosted on different floors of the same building. Spanish legendary marques such as Montesa, Bultaco and Derbi are well represented, as is an eclectic selection of MV, Ducati, Yamaha, Honda, Harley-Davidson,

Norton and Triumph. Complete, the two-wheel collection is 250 strong.

Folch likes to recall that the first car he bought on his allowances was a Seat 600, the most popular two-door, rear-engined model made in Spain. Folch started collecting cars almost by accident when a customer failed to retrieve a broken-down Lotus Elan S2 left in a workshop for repairs. Passing through the shop, the car caught the eye of Folch, who paid the bill of $500 and left at the wheel of the little plastic-bodied sports car. It was a restoration project that happily led its new owner to an interest in promoting the rescue and restoration of historical motor vehicles.

Had he to part with all his cars but one, Folch would keep the Maserati 250F for its significance in Spanish motoring history ... or the Ford GT40, because one always needs a practical road car. AQ

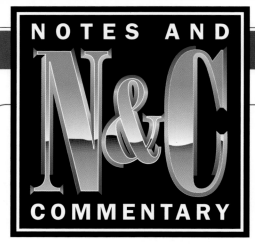

NOTES AND N&C COMMENTARY

VOLUME 48 No. 1

CONTACTING AQ

Automobile Quarterly, ISSN 0005-1438, ISBN 1-59613-057-1 (978-1-59613-057-9), is published quarterly by Automobile Heritage Publishing and Communications, LLC. Editorial and publication offices: 800 East 8th Street, New Albany, Indiana, USA 47150. Telephone (812) 948-AUTO (2886); fax (812) 948-2816; e-mail info@autoquarterly.com; Web site www.autoquarterly.com.

SUBSCRIPTION SERVICE

For subscriptions, back issues, indexes, reader service, changes of address, and order entry, call (866) 838-2886. If calling from Indiana or outside the U.S., call (812) 948-2886. Back issue prices start at $25.95, plus shipping. For domestic subscription orders: 1 year (4 issues), $79.95; 2 years (8 issues), $149.95; 3 years (12 issues), $199.95. for Canadian orders: 1 year, $99.95; 2 years, $189.95; 3 years, $259.95. For all other international orders: 1 year, $109.95; 2 years, $209.95; 3 years, $289.95. Mastercard, Visa, or American Express are accepted. Order online at www.autoquarterly.com. To order by mail, please send check or money order to *AQ/Automobile Quarterly*, 1950 Classic Car Circle, P.O. Box 1950, New Albany, IN 47151. The fax number for orders is (812) 948-2816.

POSTMASTER

Please send all changes of address to: *Automobile Quarterly*, P.O. Box 1950, New Albany, IN 47151. Periodical postage paid at New Albany, Indiana, and at additional mailing offices.

LEGAL NOTICE

Entire contents copyright 2008 by Automobile Heritage Publishing and Communications, LLC. Library of Congress Catalog Number 62-4005. *AQ, Automobile Quarterly*, Quatrafoil, and AQ are registered trademarks of Automobile Heritage Publishing and Communications, LLC. All rights reserved. Reproduction in whole or in part without permission is prohibited.

OPPORTUNITY

Details of fund raising programs for car clubs and automobile museums are available by calling: (812) 948-AUTO (2886).

Cover & Contents

Illustrations by Steve Anderson.

Frontispiece

Color photography: p.1, from the AQ Photo and Research Archives.

Studebaker's Final Days

All black-and-white photography from the collection of the author.

Color photography: pp. 4, 7 (top), 8, 9, 11, 15, 16, 17, 18, 19, 20 (top), 21 (top) from the AQ Photo and Research Archives; pp. 5, 6, 7 (bottom), 10, 20 (bottom), 21 (bottom) from the author's collection.

Studebaker National Museum

The author would like to thank Stu Chapman, Richard Quinn, Rebecca J. Bonham, Peggy Soderberg and Tony Smith for their assistance with this article.

All photography courtesy of the Studebaker National Museum.

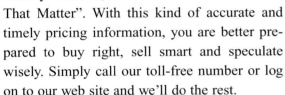

Bernd Rosemeyer

Black-and-white photography: pp. 32, 33, 34 (top), 37 (left), 38 (right). 42 (right) copyright LAT Photographic; pp. 34 (bottom), 35, 38 (left) from the National Motor Museum; p. 36 (top) from the AQ Photo and Research Archives; pp. 36 (bottom), 37 (right), 42 (left) Mercedes-Benz photo; p. 39 from the Phil Harms Collection.

Color photography: pp. 40, 41, 43 from the AQ Photo and Research Archives.

SS 90 and 100

Special thanks John Norcia for sharing his restored SS Jaguar 100 with our readers.
Color photography: pp. 44-53 from the AQ Photo and Research Archives; pp. 54, 55 by John Norcia.

Bibliography

Clark, R M, ed. *Jaguar & SS Cars 1931-1951*. Brooklands Books;
Long, Brian. *Daimler SP250*. Veloce Publishing, 1994;
Skilleter, Paul. *Jaguar Sports Cars*. G T Foulis & Co Ltd.;
Skilleter, Paul and A. Whyte. *Jaguar Sports Cars*. Foulis/Haynes, 1988;
Whyte, Andrew. *Jaguar: The history of a Great British Car*. PSL, 1980;
Various editions of *The Autocar* and *The Motor*.

Art Gallery with Steve Anderson

Color photography from the artist.

Contact Information

Steve Anderson Illustrations
P.O. Box 1991
Burbank, Ca 91507
Phone: (626) 796.8410
Fax: (626) 796.8504
E Mail: designsa@earthlink.net
Web site: www.sailllustrations.com

E.J. Hall biography

Indispensible in the creation of this project has been Jay Eitel, Hall's nephew. Years ago Eitel took possession of four file cabinets filled with Hall's personal effects, professional papers, and other invaluable bits, saving them from sure destruction. He made these materials available to me, provided a personal interview, and also answered innumerable questions. John Perala provided critical research in newspapers on Hall and Hall-Scott, and I am in great debt to Beverly Rae Kimes for steering me to John. Lorry Dunning, historical consultant, unearthed long-overlooked documents linking Hall to Holt. Howard Reinke opened up his DeVaux-Hall collection to me. Taylor Scott made available the Leland Scott (Bert's brother) family collection. Northern State University staff and administration provided release time, technical staff support, and funding to cover reproduction, equipment, and travel; especially important NSU have been Carolyn Blanchard, Taylor Ford, Linda Gray, Dave Grettler, Jackie Hanson, Bobbi Jo Rissmann, and John Romeo. This essay is an outgrowth of a book written by Francis H. Bradford and Ric A. Dias, *Hall-Scott: The Untold Story of a Great American Engine Maker*, SAE, Int'l, Warrendale, 2007. Francis Bradford created the initial spark for this project when he wrote the first full-length history of Hall-Scott, an unpublished manuscript, in the 1980s. A former Hall-Scott employee, he gave me hundreds of images, written sources, and a basic storyline of the company before he passed away in 2005.

Photography: pp. 62, 63, 68 (top right), 71 (top), 72, 73 (bottom right), 74 (right), 75 courtesy of Jay Eitel; pp. 64 (top), 65, 66 (top), 67, 68 (bottom), 69, 73 (top), courtesy of Taylor Scott; p. 66 (bottom left and right) courtesy of Old Rhinebeck Aerodrome; p. 70 (right) courtesy of Wichita State University Libraries; p. 71 (bottom) courtesy of Department of Special Collections, University of California, Davis, found by Lorry Dunning; p. 74 (left) courtesy of Howard Reinke; p. 64 (bottom) courtesy of John Perala; pp.68 (left), 70 (left), 73 (bottom left) from the author's collection.

Bibliography

Angle, Glenn, *Airplane Engine Encyclopedia*, Otterbein Press, Dayton, 1921;
Borgeson, Griffith, *The Golden Age of the American Racing Car, 2nd ed.*, SAE Int'l, Warrendale, 1998;
Bowers, Peter, *Boeing Aircraft Since 1916*, Funk and Wagnalls, New York, 1968;
Dees, Mark, *The Miller Dynasty, 2nd ed.*, Hippodrome Publishing, Moorpark, 1994;
Dickey, Philip, *The Liberty Engine 1918-1942*, Smithsonian Institution Press, Washington, 1968;
Grayson, Stan, *Engines Afloat, From Early Days to D-Day, vol. I : The Gasoline Era*, Devereux Books, Marblehead, 1999;
Heilig, John, *The Cadillac Century*, Chartwell Books, Edison, 1998;
Keilty, Edmund, *Interurbans Without Wires*, Interurbans, Glendale, 1979;
Johnson, Kenneth, *Aerial California*, Dawson's Book Shop, Los Angeles, 1961;
Kimes, Beverly Rae, ed., *Standard Catalog of American Cars, 1805-1942, 3rd edition*, Krause Publications, Iola, 1996;
Lenzke, James, ed., *Standard Catalog of Cadillac, 1903-2000*, Krause Publications, Iola, 2000;
National Cyclopaedia of American Biography, vol. XLIII, University Microfilms, Ann Arbor, 1967;
Reynolds, John, *Andre Citroen*, St. Martin's Press, New York, 1996.

London-Sydney Marathon

The following sources were used in preparation and research for this article: David McKay and J. Smailes's book *Bright Eyes of Danger*; Nick Brittan's book *Marathon: Around the World in a Cloud of Dust*; Max Stahl's articles in *Racing Car News* magazine, January-February-March 1969; Ford Motor Company of Australia; Ford Motor Company of England; Ford Motor Company of Germany; DaimlerChrysler AG archives; Prolab Fotofachlabor GmbH; Anne-Marie Michel, Citroën Archives; Bill Forsyth of Sun Photographics; John Roach,

London Sydney webmaster; Jenny Brittan; Andrew Cowan; John Smailes; Max Stahl; Ian Vaughan, John Gowland, Graham Hoinville, Garry Chapman (Australia, ex-Ford); and Bill Barnett (UK ex-Ford). Various magazines were also sourced: *Wheels, Modern Motor, Autocar, Racing Car News*.

Black-and-white photography: pp. 76, 77, 78 (top) from the *Daily Telegraph*; p. 78 (left) by John Roach; pp. 78 (bottom), 80, 81, 82, 83, 84, 86 (bottom), 87 by Bill Forsyth; pp. 79, 85 courtesy of Ford Motor Company Australia; p. 86 (top) by R. Berghouse.

Motoring at the Panama Canal
The author would like to thank the staffs of the Library of Congress in Washington, D.C., and the National Archives in College, Park, Maryland, for their help locating the photographs and text information that have made this story possible.

All photography from the National Archives.

Bibliography
Blanco, Jorge J. "Life in a Yankee Utopia." *American Mercury*, April 1932;

Bonsal, Stephen. "Life In Panama Canal Zone." *The Mentor*, February 1925;

"Canal Expose." *Literary Digest*, December 12, 1936;

Crilley, A Cyril, United States Department of Commerce Acting Commercial Attache, Panama City, Panama. Special Report No. 5. Subject: Co-ordination of Rail and Motor Transport, Panama and Canal Zone. October 13, 1933;

Gries, Samuel, jr., Motor Car Inspector, The Panama Canal, Culebra. "Memorandum to the Governor regarding automobile for the Health Department." July 31, 1914;

"New Nash Display Rooms Opened." *Star and Herald*, March 9, 1930;

"Newspaper Specials." *Wall Street Journal*, June 20, 1914;

"Panama Canal Opened." *Wall Street Journal*, August 15, 1914;

Peck, George Curtis, United States Department of Commerce Commercial Attache, Panama City, Panama. Memo to Automotive Division, Department of Commerce. Subject: Auto Agencies in Panama. February 29, 1928;

Peck, George Curtis, United States Department of Commerce Commercial Attache, Panama City, Panama. Memo to Automotive Division, Department of Commerce. Subject: Re-exports from the Canal Zone. March 20, 1929;

"Roosevelt Spends Busy Four Hours Here." *Star and Herald*, October 17, 1935;

"Roosevelt Tours Canal Zone Area." *New York Times*, August 6, 1938;

Ryden, R. W.,Superintendent, Mechanical Division, The Panama Canal. Letter to Chief, Police and Fire Division, Balboa Heights. Subject: Abandoned automobile. April 18, 1933;

"Sale Of Lindy's Stamps To Commence The Day Of His Arrival On Isthmus." *Panama American*, January 6, 1928;

Scott, L.B., Port Captain, Balboa, The Panama Canal. Memorandum For Marine Superintendent, October 26, 1933;

"65 Autos in Canal Zone." *New York Times*, September 23, 1912;

"U.S. May Finance Trans-Isthmian Highway." *Star and Herald*, October 18, 1935.

Can Costa Foundation Collection
The author would like to thank Joaquín Folch-Rusiñol Corachán, for the introduction of the Can Costa Foundation and providing information on the featured cars, as well as Jesús González, Carles Boada and Angel Solera.

All photos from the author's collection. Color photography: pp. 101, 107 of Folch at Nürburgring, August 2007, by the author; all photos at the Can Costa Foundation taken in March 2008, by Studio Pascucci.

Bibliography
Automobile Quarterly, Vol. 25 No. 3 and Vol. 32 No. 3;

Bianchi Anderloni, Carlo Felice and Anselmi, Angelo. *Carrozzeria Touring*. Autocritica: Roma, 1982;

Coma-Cros, Enrique. *Escudería Montjuich*. Barcelona, 1999;

Crombac, Gérard. *Sport-Auto* (F), various issues;

del Arco de Izco, Javier, *40 Años de historia del automovilismo en el circuito de Montjuïc*. Can Costa Foundation, Barcelona, 2000;

Henry, Alan. *Brabham*. ACLA: Paris, 1985;

Laguna, Mario. *La aventura Pegaso*. Virton (B), 2006;

L'Année Automobile (CH), various issues;

Mirabent, Antoni. *Autódromo Nacional*. Sitges (E) 1999;

Nye, Doug. *McLaren*. ACLA: Paris 1984.

Coda
Color photography courtesy of Reeves Callaway.

Back Cover
Debossment of the Studebaker logo from the AQ Photo and Research Archive.

Errata, Changes & Updates
Many thanks to L.G. Séchy for pointing out corrections in the article on the Serenissima Jet Competizine in Vol. 47 No. 2. The correct designation for the featured model does not include "308." The correct time recording on p. 98 is "4.18.2" instead of "four hours 18.2 minutes" that was ahead of the GTO of A. de Cortanze/G. Larrousse, which was not Volpi's old Ferrari. On p. 101: the Aghema GT is actually the Agena GT; that a Jaguar V-8 was used in any Serenissima or Agena is suspect, as records show that these models were under Serenissima power throughout; records show that no Serenissima engine was used during McLaren's Monza tests; and P. Drogo is, in fact, Piero Drogo Carrozeria Sports Cars, Modena.

A Gunslinger's Hot Rod

Of all the fast machines roaring out of Callaway's engineering labs and garages these past 30 years, one stands out in its beckoning to an earlier age: a 1928 Stutz BB four-passenger Black Hawk speedster powered by a 1931 Stutz DV32 engine. It was a memorable commission – reportedly costing about $300,000 – from a memorable person.

William Ruger Sr., of arms making fame, was in love with the Stutz DV32 in his youth. In 1995, he challenged Callaway Advanced Technology with the assignment: If you were Harry Stutz, and you suddenly awakened knowing what is now known about engine technology, what would you do to the DV32? The result was a turbocharged, fuel-injected version of the 5.0-liter dohc straight-eight that makes more than 300 bhp at 3800 rpm. The modernized engine drives a GM Turbo Hydramatic 4L80E – suitable power and torque for a 6,000-pound automobile.

Forbes once described Ruger as "the tweedy, brushy-mustached sportsman-industrialist" and a cross between Teddy Roosevelt and Ernest Hemingway, while noting the uncanny ability of his Sturm, Ruger & Co. to prosper even as the gun industry slipped. A tireless and self-taught engineer, Ruger's name was mentioned in the same conversations as Samuel Colt and John Browning.

It's interesting to note that the Ruger "Bearcat" .22 single-action revolver was first announced in the August 1958 issue of the National Rifle Association's *American Rifleman* magazine. It is said that Ruger named this revolver after his favorite automobile.

"Bill was an iconic, determined, single-minded, I'll-do-it-my-way kind of guy," said Reeves Callaway. "He viewed the Stutz as the sports car of his youth. It was the Corvette of the times."

The Stutz's rebuilt engine came equipped with nine steel-backed shell main bearings, forged aluminum pistons, stainless steel valves, and titanium connecting rods (forged at Sturm Ruger). A Garrett TO4B turbocharger provides 17 psi boost, with Motec engine management and Callaway software controlling sequential port injectors.

For this project alone we agree with Alan Farnham, who noted in *Forbes Life*: "In cars, as in the firearms he made, Bill Ruger prized fine engineering above all else." AQ

ML   7/08